Nathan Shaw addresses an area
ment, prophets thundered agai
and fatherless. For example, Isa
for the widow." The apostle Jan
God's heart in James 1:27: "Pure and undefiled religion in the sight of our
God and Father is this: to visit orphans and widows in their distress. . . ."
Nathan makes us painfully aware how we have not only not succored
widows and orphans, but we have actually increased their sufferings by
our judgments, both expressed and undercurrent.

Christian hearts need to hear this message and repent. If we are to
advance into the climactic adventures and warfare of the end times, Nathan Shaw well says that it is those who have known abandonment who
will best be able to lead us in the coming days.

John Loren Sandford, co-founder, Elijah House, Inc.

Nathan has captured a revelation of the heartbeat of God for the plight
of God's precious people—the divorcees, widows and fatherless who have
been neglected, judged and forsaken. Through his skillful use of God's
Word coupled with examples from real life, Nathan brings a plumbline of
truth to confront and challenge the religious attitudes and belief systems
of our day. His keen sensitivity and insights mirror God's loving nature
and bring a triumphant message of hope and grace. Although Nathan
champions divorcees, widows and the fatherless, this prophetic message
to the Church encompasses men *and* women, challenging all our broken
vessels to become ones that honor each other and King Jesus.

Jill Austin, president and founder, Master Potter Ministries

Psalm 102:17 expresses God's heart when it says, "He shall regard the
prayer of the destitute, and shall not despise their prayer" (NKJV). Nathan
Shaw expresses the same heart cry of God for the destitute and despised.
Unto the Least of These is a clarion call for us to draw near to God and let
His concern become our concern. I highly recommend it as a cutting-edge
message for the twenty-first century.

Mike Bickle, director, International House of Prayer,
Kansas City, Missouri

The greatest assault in our day is not from terrorists who scheme against
us in the public streets; it is the terrible private war that goes on daily
against the God-honoring ancient bonds of marriage and home. In a day
of broken dreams, shattered friendships and fractured families, Nathan
Shaw's unique and insightful treatment brings practical and biblical help
to those who have been hurt from the pain of separation, abandonment
or betrayed covenants.

Ancient prophecy spoke of a day in which special favor from heaven
would grace five enemy targets: children, young people, the elderly, servant
workers and women. For all who have been affected in some way by family
breakup or loss, and for those who have to deal with the sad twenty-first

century reality of homes hurt, broken or under attack, *Unto the Least of These* is a must-read, can-do, God's-promise priority book.

Winkie Pratney, author, speaker

This book well handles the balance between the problem and the solution. Shaw understands the hurts and suffering of the single life while teaching ways to rise above them and succeed. Leaders may well find their counseling load reduced by sharing this book with counselees. I recommend it.

Iverna Tompkins, president, Iverna Tompkins Ministries, Scottsdale, Arizona

The Church in the Western world is facing a crisis—a rapidly growing number of people who are either divorced, widowed or facing the pain of dysfunctional relationships. God has set a place for them (like all who enter the Church) to settle in and has given them a destiny to fulfill. But their pain is often enhanced when they come to church and feel isolated and rejected. Nathan's book is a prophetic call for the Church to wake up to the needs of people desperate to find identity and meaning. He calls the Church back to her responsibility to support and minister to widows, orphans, the fatherless. He also brings practical encouragement and advice to those who have suffered the indignities of a failed marriage or broken relationship. The issues raised in *Unto the Least of These* are important for the future health of the Body of Christ.

Brent Douglas, senior leader, Encounter Christian Center, Auckland, New Zealand

With our society so full of painfully wounded people lacking the blessing of a father, it is a breath of fresh air to see principles of covenant and restoration laid out so systematically. Psalm 68:5 says, "God will be a father to the fatherless and a defender of widows." Nathan Shaw shows how God is rebuilding the lives of divorcees, widows and the fatherless through a revelation of the Father's love.

Dr. Gary Greenwald, founder, Eagle's Nest Ministries, Santa Ana, California

My heart was warmed by the compassion and love that I (coming from a broken home and raised by a single mother) felt when I read *Unto the Least of These*. This book will bring healing to those with holes in their souls.

John A. Kilpatrick, senior pastor, Brownsville Assembly of God, Pensacola, Florida

This book will bless many. Nathan deals with the age-long struggle between religious idealism and the realism that God's people face today. The Father heart of God is restoration and healing. These are the days of the fulfillment of Malachi 4:5–6, when restoration is taking place in individuals, marriages, families and the Church. Thank God for a prophetic book that gives a vision and hope for the future! The truths contained in *Unto the Least of These* will enable all believers, regardless of their personal status, to prosper personally and in their ministries in Christ. Thank you, Nathan, for revealing the heart of God to His people.

Dr. Bill Hamon, chairman and founder, Christian International Ministries Network, Santa Rosa Beach, Florida

I am glad this topic is being approached from a biblical perspective. We need a compassionate, redemptive solution for the many who have been trying to relate. I pray this book will be used to encourage all the Church.

Dudley Hall, founder and president, Successful Christian Living Ministries, Euless, Texas

The topic of this book is far too rare! Rather than having a theme of self-improvement, it addresses the needs of others and how to minister to them. Nathan Shaw unveils the plight of countless thousands within the Body of Christ whose needs are ignored or unmet. It is time for the Church to focus once again on what "pure religion" is all about. This book is both insightful and biblical and challenges the very core of our beliefs and responsibilities. I highly recommend it to you.

David Ravenhill, teacher, Lindale, Texas

More than anything else, the pages of this book communicated God's love and tenderness toward me. They gave me the courage to let go of being a victim and reach for a destiny in God beyond anything I dreamed possible. This book restored me and gave me hope. I wish it had been around ten years ago when I went through the devastation of divorce.

Sue Nesbit, divorcee, mother of two

When all is said and done, the Bible always brings us back to God's relentless insistence that how we treat the "least" is a key measure of our faithfulness. Nathan has written a passionate and timely book.

Rob Harley, Christian writer and broadcaster

The current rise in divorce rates throughout the Western world is a problem with enormous social consequences. The greatest legacy we can give future generations is the concept of two-parent families. In the dearth of practical advice for those facing marriage or relationship trauma, Nathan's book shows clearly that the Bible gives distinct guidance and a clear way. I commend this book not only to those having relationship problems but to all people with marriages and families, whether in trouble or not.

Dick Hubbard, founder, Hubbard Foods, Ltd.

I was delighted to read Nathan Shaw's book *Unto the Least of These*. First, it draws attention to the many references to the heart of God for women who are left alone. Mr. Shaw refers to many passages in the Old Testament in which orphans and widows are given special mention—far more than most people realize. And he is right to enlarge God's concern to cover other dispossessed women, such as divorcees and abandoned partners. Second, I was impressed that a man, and a relatively young man, should show such understanding of and empathy with the thoughts and feelings of today's abandoned women. It can only be because God has laid such a concern on his heart. Third, his concern is not only for those suffering abandonment or loss, but also for the Church as a whole, whose attitudes are so often critical of the sufferer and lacking the special care, protection and help God requires His people to show to orphans and widows in their midst. Fourth, the book is peppered with biblical stories and comments, which are carefully considered for the lessons he draws. May this book be widely read and prove a blessing to many.

The Rev. Dr. David Stewart, principal,
The Bible College of New Zealand, 1965–1988

The topic of this book is both timely and necessary to address the condemnation felt by people afflicted by divorce and family breakup. Many people we have dealt with over the years have had huge burdens of shame and very little hope. This book blesses people with a great message of hope to enter into God's will for their lives. A significant ministry tool for counselors, church workers and friends of those affected by this crisis in our society.

Trevor Yaxley, co-founder, Lifeway Ministries,
Auckland, New Zealand

UNTO *the* LEAST *of* THESE

Expressing God's Love
to Widows and the Fatherless

Nathan Shaw

Chosen Books

A Division of Baker Book House Co
Grand Rapids, Michigan 49516

Published by Chosen Books
a division of Baker Book House Company
P.O. Box 6287, Grand Rapids, MI 49516-6287
www.bakerbooks.com

Printed in the United States of America

Library of Congress Cataloging-in-Publication Data
Shaw, Nathan.
    Unto the least of these : expressing God's love to widows and the
fatherless / Nathan Shaw.
        p.   cm.
    ISBN 0-8007-9344-7 (pbk.)
    1. Church work with widows. 2. Church work with orphans.
    I. Title.
    BV4445.S48 2004
    259'.6—dc22   2003015943

To Sue Nesbit and all those like her
who have had to fight alone.

With love.

Contents

Acknowledgments

My mum, Avis Shaw, for turning my messy writing into a typed manuscript.

The Rev. Dr. David Stewart, John Sandford and my dad, Cam Shaw, for their comments, suggestions and editing, most of which were done on airplanes, between meetings and in the midst of busy schedules.

Jane Campbell, editorial director of Chosen Books, for being patient and kind with this rather over-enthusiastic first-time author.

Ann Weinheimer for the superb job of polishing and shaping the final manuscript.

And, finally, a big thank you to the divorcees, widows and fatherless who shared their lives and their stories with me.

Introduction

Jesus sat watching as people put their offerings into the Temple treasury. Along came a widow who dropped in two mites. A mite—the smallest coin in circulation at the time. According to Jesus this woman put in more than all the others because it was all she had. He commended her for her wholeheartedness.

It is no secret that Jesus esteemed and honored widows. In fact every truly righteous individual represented in the Bible, from Genesis to Revelation, did the same. And not just widows, of course: The story of the two mites carries a message of hope for all of those in every generation who suffer broken and destitute lives. Thus, in writing this book I have endeavored to heed the biblical exhortation that calls on us to help those who have been relationally abandoned: "Defend the fatherless, plead for the widow" (Isaiah 1:17).

This is in keeping with Jesus' own life and works. When Jesus came to the nation of Israel, His ministry was motivated by His heart of compassion and mercy for a people who had no shepherd and hence no protection and nurture.

Look, for example, at the three stories in the gospels in which Jesus raised someone from the dead. They involve:

A widow's son (see Luke 7:11–17)
Jairus' daughter (see Luke 8:40–56)
Lazarus (see John 11:1–44)

While each reveals Jesus' mercy and compassion, the first story about the grieving widow shows us much about His heart in relation to the lonely and destitute. In the two other stories about Jairus and Lazarus, Jesus was sought out and asked to come and help. With the widow, however, Jesus took the initiative by intercepting her son's funeral procession. Jesus went on a specific assignment: turning to a widow in a time of great need. Because this woman had only one son, there was no way for her husband's lineage to continue. She also had no one to care and provide for her in a society that offered very little to those without means.

This is a striking message for the Church today, for it shows us something of the Father's heart as well: Remember, Jesus did only what He saw the Father doing. Understanding the Father's heart for broken and destitute lives—and obeying His call on our own hearts—is going to result in His miraculous power being manifest in unprecedented ways.

The mysteries and treasures hidden in God's dealings with widows and the fatherless are profound. And those mysteries will be revealed only as we put ourselves in the shoes of the broken and destitute. In fact, understanding God's message about the broken and destitute is crucial for bringing the Church to the level of maturity needed to fulfill her end-time mandate. Or, to put it another way, misunderstanding this subject is one of the main reasons for the present level of immaturity within our ranks. It is critical that the Church grow in this area if she is to walk in the fullness of her apostolic calling.

Do we feel the heartbeat of societies ripped apart by the devastation of divorce, abuse, sexual immorality? No one can miss the fact that breakdown of the family unit in much of the Western world has reached unimaginable proportions; the very moral fiber of our nations is coming apart at the seams. In my native country, New Zealand, which has four million people, there are on average almost two hundred divorces every week. Half of all births occur outside of marriage. In the United States there are on average about 22,000 divorces every week; and one-third of all births occur outside of marriage.

Every day we come into contact with those who face devastation: the loss of a husband, wife, father or mother; the job of rearing a child by a mom or dad who has never been married; the hurt of living in a home with a father who abdicates his role; the feelings within a marriage of aloneness and isolation; the grief of a troubled marriage that is on the brink of disaster.

If revival is to have impact on a nation, it must reach to the very heart of that nation. It is time to wake up and reach out with the Father's compassion. As the Church, until we do this, we fail to be relevant.

Some portions of this book deal with the contrast between the present condition of the Body of Christ and that to which she is called. Please understand that it is not my intention to be critical of the present situation but simply to acknowledge reality. What I have written comes from a heart devoted to love for the truth. It is born out of deep love for Christ's Body, the Church. True love will not compromise the biblical standard. It will, however, restore hope in God's willingness to empower us to live as He has ordained.

Note that I have applied the Scriptures about widows to divorcees as well. According to Deuteronomy 24:1–4 some widows in Israel would have been divorcees (see also 1 Corinthians 7:15). The prophets in the Old Testament repeatedly reminded the Israelites to care for widows, orphans and strangers (foreigners). This must have included divorcees, as their plight was not very different (in fact, it was worse) from those widowed through death of a spouse. When the Bible refers to widows, orphans and foreigners, it is referring to those who are most needy.

In describing the plight of widows and divorcees, I am in no way limiting the message to women. Generally men are more likely to be the spouse to die first because they marry older, have a shorter life expectancy and have more work-related accidents resulting in death. It is also more common for men to desert women and children than the other way around. Nevertheless, when the truths herein apply to men, please receive them as such. God calls us as His Church to restore honor and dignity to all who are hurting.

Here is a story that illustrates the journey we will be taking together in this book. It is inevitable, you see, that as we hear and minister to the cries of the wounded, we will likely face the wounding in our own hearts. Like me, perhaps you have felt stuck in a "pit" of emotional pain, helpless and with no way to get out. As I have ministered to people around me, I have heard many similar stories—the most heart-wrenching ones told by those in broken relationships. I have written the following story to help illustrate and describe their plight. It is the voice of one solitary figure, trapped in a pit of emotional pain.

There was no way out. I was stuck in a very large pit. This had to be the cruelest blow of my life. A lot of people happened upon the edge of my pit as they went about their lives. As I sat there, I began to realize that the people who approached the edge of my pit fit into a number of categories.

First were those who were blind to the pit. They could see some things but not the enormous crater in which I dwelt. Despite the fact that I cried out for help, they just looked at me, puzzled, as if to say, "What's wrong?" It amazed me that they never fell in head over heels and joined me, out of sheer carelessness and negligence.

Next were those who could see the pit but kept their hands firmly over their ears, blocking out my plaintive cry. When they first heard my cry, a look of terror crossed their faces. Fear of facing unhealed hurts, which my predicament was exposing, caused them to clap their hands over their ears so fast that I was surprised they did not knock themselves out! At the same time they usually shouted out a comment designed to shut me up. Yes, a lot of these comments were religious platitudes and verses from the Bible and were uttered from the mouths of well-meaning Christians.

The most energetic people were the ones who ran up to the edge of my pit, put their hands to their mouths, shouted something at me and then ran off. They looked as though they were on a mission to save the earth and were absolutely convinced that their advice would lift me out of the pit. When they came back and found me still there, they shouted louder and sometimes made comments about my character, explaining how I was blocking their advice from working. How I wished they would use their frenzied efforts to help lift me out! Did they not see that I could use a hand? They acted as if the strength of their words was going to catapult me out.

There were some merciful souls who saw me but just stood at the edge of the pit and looked helpless. They would have helped me if they could have, but they did not seem to know how. They wept for me, but their sympathy, the tears pouring from their hearts of gold, simply dropped to the ground.

Then there were the overly fearful. They came together and carefully consulted about how to help me. They spent a lot of time checking the edge of the pit to see how secure it was, so that they could fasten safety equipment to it. They were treating the edge of my pit as though it were a cliff face; they were being very cautious. They reasoned that if they fell into the pit with me, they would not be able to help me out. I could hear their reasoning: "If a person falls over a cliff and half kills himself, what help is he going to be? There's no point rushing in carelessly and winding up a second casualty."

Finally this group of overly fearful decided the safety equipment was secure enough for someone to abseil into the pit. This led to a serious discussion about protocol: Who was the appropriate one to go? It would most certainly be inappropriate, they agreed, to send someone who was of the opposite sex or had experienced moral failings in the past. Finally the very well-selected person began his descent. After going a short distance he slipped. They hauled him out with the safety rope and gave him the ministry I needed. He was quite shaken and by this time his fear had spread to everyone else.

It was painful to see group after group—including some of my close friends—turning their backs on me.

After I had remained in the pit for longer than I could imagine possible, somebody finally came along who could help me. He looked as though he was on a mission, an assignment from the King, but he did not look frantic. His heart was full of compassion and he wept for me, but he also had the confidence to climb into the pit and weep with me. He descended the wall of the pit with relative ease, making the former abseil attempt look rather ridiculous.

He came over and gently put his arm around me. I had not been touched with genuine compassion for a very long time. My heart had become hardened. Gently he imparted strength, which encouraged me and opened me to receiving his help. He guided me, one step at a time, and was patient day after day, week after week, month after month as I climbed up and approached restoration.

Sometimes the people returned to the edge of the pit and criticized both me and my helper, but their taunts became less and less powerful as trust was restored in my heart. Finally I emerged with one final heave, over the top, full, healthy and whole.

Now, many of the people who had tried to help me began looking to me to help them.

What does it mean to be widowed or fatherless? For most it is a devastating crisis of identity, security and survival. I invite you, through the pages of this book, to journey with me as we discover God's heart and passion to restore these broken lives.

Part 1

A Biblical Perspective

one

Desolate Places

*Sophie had been married five years and had two small
children when her husband had a stroke. He was
left partially paralyzed and his personality changed
dramatically. He was no longer the caring husband and
father that he once was. About fifteen years later he had
another stroke, which greatly affected his mind. Because
of this he had to go into a 24-hour care facility. Even
though Sophie's husband was still alive, she had been
effectively widowed. Emotionally she was overwhelmed
with loneliness as well as grief and anger—and guilt
for putting him into a facility. It was particularly hard
for her to watch her teenage son and daughter come to
terms with no longer having their father at home. The
few instances when her husband realized he was not
going home, he tried to hit Sophie with his walking
stick. At the time of writing he has a tumor and only a
short time to live.*

*Shelley's world as well as her theology were
completely shattered when, without warning, her*

Christian husband left her for another woman. After fourteen years of marriage she was left to bring up their two young girls on her own. She bore not only the shame of being replaced by another woman but also judgment from fellow Christians and her children for her husband's departure.

Marie's life changed dramatically when her father left. As a young girl she felt responsible for the separation and divorce that followed. She tried to fill the role of her father as best she could by comforting and supporting her mother and mothering her younger sister. For years her heart ached to have a father. As the years dragged on without a fulfillment of this desire, she found herself increasingly having to cope with depression and thoughts of suicide. As a teenager she repeatedly pursued relationships with boys to fill the void left in her life by her father's absence.

Grace had been married 34 years when her husband, Eric, died of cancer. The first eighteen years of their marriage had been very turbulent. When they both become Christians, however, God completely transformed their marriage. They became a great team and did everything together. During the last seven years of their marriage they had a teaching ministry to the nations. It was hard for Grace to understand why God would go to so much trouble to help her become one with her husband, then leave her on her own to become whole again. Not only had she lost her husband and closest friend, but also her ministry, as many in the church who accepted her calling as a married woman rejected her as a woman in ministry on her own. She did not know who she was anymore, nor did she feel that she was of value to anyone.

Today we live in a world in which broken relationships spew their carnage all about us. The widows and fatherless—and by implication all those who are oppressed and without the financial, emotional or physical resources to protect and help themselves—are particularly vulnerable to the abuses of a society that does not recognize their plight. It is into such lives that the Church is called to bring hope, order and restoration. It is a calling rich with God's own compassion and mercy.

Widow Defined

In order to help us come to a greater understanding of this concept of relational brokenness that widows and the fatherless often suffer, let us start by having a look at the meaning of the word translated "widow" in the Bible.

The Old Testament word for *widow* is *almanah*. This word could also be used to refer to a desolate place or house. This provides us with what I believe to be a good word picture of what it is like to be a widow in need. Imagine the house you now live in stripped of every piece of furniture, every decoration. Then take out all the curtains, the carpet, the wallpaper and the insulation. Cut off the water supply and the electricity and imagine this house placed in the barren and hostile Antarctic—an apt image of the coldness of heart. What is left? I think *desolation* would aptly describe such a house.

How would you feel waking up in such a house each morning? How would you feel living there every moment of the day until sleep finally took you from the reality of your surroundings? Now you may begin to have some comprehension of what it is to be a distressed and destitute widow.

The New Testament word for *widow* is *chera,* which comes from the word *chasma,* meaning "a chasm or gulf." Emotionally, a widow feels a vacancy so large it can only be described as a chasm or gulf.

While it is true that in some instances widows and the fatherless of today fare better than their counterparts in biblical times, it should be noted that there were rich widows even then. Scriptures about widows and the fatherless refer to the many who are physically impoverished, but perhaps more importantly they also include the relational impoverishment that extends to almost all widows and the fatherless.

The Bible says that in marriage two become one (see 1 Corinthians 6:16). How strong must a bond be to make two separate entities into one? Very strong! Hence breaking that bond, through death or divorce, feels like cutting off part of oneself. In fact, one of the words used for *divorce* in the Old Testament, *keriythuwth*, means "a cutting of the marriage bond." The bond created between a man and a woman through marriage is so strong that the only way to be free from it is to cut it. Those who face such a cutting of two souls that have been bonded together compare it to cutting one of your limbs off, or, as one woman told me, it felt like cutting her heart in half.

The word *keriythuwth*, which comes from the word *karath* meaning "to cut," is used with reference to an ancient blood covenant that was sealed by cutting flesh (of an animal) and passing between the two pieces. Covenants are the most serious, solemn agreements in the Bible and they were always accompanied by some form of cutting. Circumcision, for example, represents covenant with God. It involves the cutting away of a sensitive piece of flesh. Marriage is a covenant between a man and a woman. The marriage covenant is sealed by physical intimacy during which the hymen of the woman tears, causing it to bleed. It is easy to see now why we have the term "cut a covenant." Someone or something is cut, symbolizing the pouring out of one life for the other. Remember, the life is in the blood (see Leviticus 17:11).

For the most part the modern world finds it hard to comprehend the seriousness of covenants, something integral to the Christian life. Nevertheless, if a covenant is so serious it requires some form of cutting to seal it, then it must be a serious thing indeed to sever the covenant bond.

God Himself does not spare language when He describes widowhood. In Lamentations 1:1 He likens Jerusalem to a widow: "How lonely sits the city that was full of people! How like a widow is she, who was great among the nations! The princess among the provinces has become a slave!"

Jerusalem could not have been in a more desolate state. The city had been ravaged with mass slaughter and burned down, while a remnant was led off into exile. Starving mothers ate their own children while the city was under siege. This situation is likened to widowhood and expounded upon throughout the rest of the book of Lamentations.

Fatherless **Defined**

We also find in Lamentations the fact that the plight of the fatherless is similar to that of widows: "We have become orphans and fatherless" (5:3, NIV). The word for *orphans* describes the lonely or bereaved. The word for *fatherless* comes from two words, *ab* meaning "father" and *ayin* meaning "to be nothing or not exist, a nonentity." The word *ayin* is used to indicate the absence of the father. Because a child's identity is intricately linked to the relationship with his or her father, the definition of *ayin* could as easily apply to the fatherless child.

According to God's economy, children should be conceived within the bonds of a marital covenant relationship. I believe that the spirit of a child knows whether or not he or she has been conceived within the safety and protection of covenant. Whether a marital covenant has been formed or not, however, sexual intercourse is a covenantal act. Although conception may occur without the covenant of marriage, it forms a bond between parent and child that is supposed to be covenantal. The breaking of this bond by the father's—or mother's—death or desertion is as serious as any other described in this chapter.

A child knows to whom he or she belongs. That is why the concept of fatherlessness (which in our society is more prevalent than the loss of the mother) is so devastating. This knowing is deeper than conscious knowledge; after all, something of who the father is has become part of who the child is. Conception is the start of a growing relationship between father and child. If this is cut off, the spirit of the child experiences a gaping void similar to that of a widow. This is accentuated by the fact that children are dependent on their parents to grow and develop into the persons God made them to be. For a child, parents are all-powerful. Such a loss is incalculable to his growth and development.

This is often part of the reason why fatherless children exhibit rebellious behaviors: They hold anger in their hearts toward their dads for abandoning them through death, divorce or emotional distance. I have come to believe that the relationship with a father is more important than any other earthly relationship for a child.

The book of Lamentations gives a better understanding of their plight, as do many other Scriptures. As I noted in the introduction, the treatment of widows and orphans is mentioned throughout the Bible. Generally, these are admonishments and they fall into two categories: how to treat widows and orphans and how *not* to treat widows and orphans. As we will see throughout this book, our attitudes have a huge impact on those living in desolate places. We continue with the issue of judgment in the next chapter.

two

Do Not Afflict

When God gave Moses laws for governing His people, He included explicit instructions for treatment of the widowed or fatherless individual.

> "You shall not afflict any widow or fatherless child. If you afflict them in any way, and they cry at all to Me, I will surely hear their cry; and My wrath will become hot, and I will kill you with the sword; your wives shall be widows, and your children fatherless."
>
> Exodus 22:22–24

God did not leave any room for doubt in this passage! Anyone who afflicts these vulnerable individuals will incur His wrath. The Hebrew word used for *afflict* is *anah*. Some of the meanings for this word are "to look down on, depress, defile, force, humble, hurt, ravish, weaken." In other words, if we put ourselves in the place of judge by looking down on others, we are not only missing an opportunity for service but disobeying God's clear command.

The Pharisaical Attitude

We understand what it is for a farmyard of chickens to have a pecking order, but too rarely do we discern such a thing among ourselves. In the Western world we may not have a caste system such as in India, but in many subtle forms it does exist. Step into church, for example, on Sunday morning and have a look around. Is there anyone you see who you feel is inferior to you? If you are honest, most likely the answer is yes. Most of us would not likely verbalize these feelings and attitudes, but we know that they are true.

Because we are "nice Christians," of course, we cover up much of these signals and actually pretend to be the opposite toward such people. The problem is this: If you are consistently at the top of the pecking order, you probably will not even notice it. If you are consistently at the bottom, however, you will pick up everyone's signals loud and clear. Widows and fatherless children fall consistently in the lowest category. Jesus talked about this in Luke 18:9–14:

> Also He spoke this parable to some who trusted in themselves that they were righteous, and despised others: "Two men went up to the temple to pray, one a Pharisee and the other a tax collector. The Pharisee stood and prayed thus with himself, 'God, I thank You that I am not like other men—extortioners, unjust, adulterers, or even as this tax collector. I fast twice a week; I give tithes of all that I possess.' And the tax collector, standing afar off, would not so much as raise his eyes to heaven, but beat his breast, saying, 'God be merciful to me a sinner!' I tell you, this man went down to

29

his house justified rather than the other; for everyone who exalts himself will be abased, and he who humbles himself will be exalted."

The Pharisee exalted himself and looked down on others. The reason he looked down on others was mainly because of what they did or did not do. Judgments and attitudes such as these are many and varied and are commonly cast upon widows and the fatherless. Divorcees are another group of hurting individuals who are judged freely and vociferously. We will discuss the plight of divorcees in a later chapter, but for now let me say that many divorcees—particularly women—suffer from unfair and ignorant accusations.

A wife, for instance, can do everything possible to nurture, support and satisfy her husband sexually, and he may still break the covenant and leave. A husband may try to be a good provider and help meet his wife's needs, but she may tire of the relationship and want out. I call many of the judgments divorcees receive the "if onlys." "If only she had been a better partner in bed." "If only she hadn't been so strong-willed." "If only he had worked harder in the marriage." The problem with all judgments is that they are made without fully knowing who the person is and where he or she has come from. God's judgment is like a sliding scale. If you have received much, much is required (see Luke 12:48). If you have received little, less is required. Only God can know the full extent of a life in order to judge fairly.

Less obvious to most are the attitudes that many widows live with after the deaths of their spouses. Often women on their own—and this includes, of course, women who have never married—are treated like second-rate citizens. Over the years my father has helped a number of widows by servicing their cars. He has ob-

30

served not only that single women are often overcharged for work done on their cars or charged for service that has not been given, but also that the work is often performed at a sub-standard level.

Women who were active in ministry with their husbands often find themselves slighted or ignored because they have no "covering" after he is gone. Some widowed women have to join the work force in order to survive, a daunting task for those who are untrained or ill-equipped. Younger women have the task of raising children alone. Older women struggle with the fear of facing the future alone at a time in life when failing strength and health take their tolls.

The fatherless are so often expected to measure up to societal norms and are judged mercilessly when they do not. They may, for example, appear antisocial or inattentive or their actions may show a lack of conscience and respect for others and for themselves. What they are missing is one of the most foundational building blocks of life.

A child who loses a father has to cope with the grief of such a huge loss without the very one who could have been the greatest support in the processing of that grief. Unprocessed grief can result in an inability to concentrate and, among other consequences, cause poor grades at school. Maybe the wayward behavior is the means of expressing a heart that is screaming out for loving attention. If this child receives judgment, the pain only increases.

It is important to remember that conscience, boundaries, confidence and healthy social skills are all developed by interacting with loving but firm role models. It is fathers in particular who express love with an unwavering firmness that brings security and strength of character.

Widows and the fatherless have a lot to contend with; God does not want us to add to their misery. Consider the things that have been taken from them: husband or father (spiritual covering, provider, leader, comforter, protector, refuge, handyman, decision-maker, friend, helper, supporter), social standing or position, intimacy, security, emotional nurture, strength. For the divorcee and her children this list also includes reputation, privacy, self-respect, confidence, trust.

In addition a single woman struggling with these issues already feels that she is failing in three important areas of her life:

- Parenting. Single parents have much to contend with in this area as they are required to fill the hole of the missing parent to the best of their ability while they themselves are in a weakened state. Divorced parents often find themselves in a losing battle, trying to set standards only to have them undone when the children visit the other parent.

- Financial management. It is easy to judge people for not keeping on top of their finances, but when you are in grief things like this often go to the side. This can happen to the best financial managers. There is a difference between neglect caused by depression and financial mismanagement.

- Emotional stability. The loss of a spouse is huge. The process of grieving will most likely be extensive and extend over a long period of time. We will discuss this fully in chapter 12. Widows, divorcees and single mothers often experience chronic loneliness. This is caused by both the absence of a marriage partner and the burden of carrying full responsibility on their own.

Looking Down or Looking Up?

Some people carry authority in such a way as to make others feel very small. Is this true of you and me? If so, we are not following the example of our Lord. From what we read about Jesus, the opposite was true. Jesus did not look down on people. He confronted supercilious religious attitudes and those who were propagating them but treated people with utmost solicitude and sensitivity.

Jesus hung out with the people who were considered the "low lifes" of the day. In fact He seemed to draw them. Being with Jesus would mean feeling utterly convicted of truth and yet, at the same time, utterly loved. There was no element of condescension in His attitude. The people He most consistently condemned were, in fact, those who maintained an attitude of superiority, the Pharisees.

One of the biggest tests of our maturity is whether or not people are drawn to us and want to be around us because they feel loved for who they are rather than for what they do. Do people want to be around us? Or can they sense we do not want to be seen with them because of what others will think of us? If we are not going to look down on others we have to either look them in the face on an equal level (this requires vulnerability) or look up to them, esteem them and see them as the incredible handiwork of God that they are. God tells us to pay special attention to widows and the fatherless because they most need it.

We dare not fail Him.

three

The Courtroom of Life

The image of a courtroom may not be one that we commonly associate with widows and orphans. It is, however, the most common imagery used when God talks about these topics in Scripture. The verse we considered in Exodus about not afflicting widows and the fatherless is the first verse to address the topic. The next verse of importance is Deuteronomy 10:18:

> "[God] administers justice for the fatherless and the widow, and loves the stranger, giving him food and clothing."

This verse differs from the one in Exodus in that it is an affirmation of God's love for the bereft as opposed to a stern command for those who would harm these relationally vulnerable people. Strong's Hebrew dictionary defines the word *justice* as "a verdict (favorable) pronounced judicially, especially a sentence or formal decree including the act, the place, the suit, the crime and the penalty; abstract justice, including participants' right or privilege."

When you think about it, life is very much like a courtroom. The people who speak for and against you are the people your life touches in one way or the other. Sometimes it feels as though life is hurling verdicts, assessments and judgments at you from many varied sources; being in court can be a traumatic experience.

We know, however, that the final assessor of our lives will be God—and He is far from passive in the trials we face. His is the only assessment that really matters. Satan, in his role as accuser of the brethren, works overtime to make us think that God is against us, thus cutting us off from the hope of a fair trial. He works hard and succeeds much of the time. What widows and the fatherless need to know above all else is that God is *for* them (see Romans 8:31). He takes interest in every aspect of their lives. "The LORD will watch over your coming and going both now and forevermore" (Psalm 121:8, NIV).

Look at God's character. The verses preceding Deuteronomy 10:18 give us an indication of how great God is.

> "Indeed heaven and the highest heavens belong to the LORD your God, also the earth with all that is in it. . . . For the LORD your God is God of gods and Lord of lords, the great God, mighty and awesome, who shows no partiality nor takes a bribe."
>
> Deuteronomy 10:14, 17

Verse 18 goes on to tell us about the specific outworking of that greatness. It tells us not only who He is, but what He does.

Someone can hold a high position—for example, the manager of a prestigious bank. He may display many letters after his name, but that does not tell us anything about his character. If, however, you learn about the bank manager's generosity and his specific fair dealings with people, you now know something about his nature. After these passages extol who God is, in all His greatness, the single attribute of His nature mentioned is that of being committed to justice. And the specific outworking of His justice is toward the widow, fatherless and stranger. God shows particular favor to those who need it most.

Israel was to remember the kindness shown to her by God. He chose her out of all the nations on earth to be His people. What is more, He chose her because she was the least (see Deuteronomy 7:6–8). God chooses every one of us because of our utter helplessness and hopelessness, not because of any merit of our own. We likewise are to choose to love those who are the least—the weak, the helpless and the hopeless.

Because of God's heart of mercy toward victims of abandonment, they can trust in these promises:

1. God is for them (see Romans 8:31).
2. He watches over every detail of their lives, missing nothing (see Psalm 121:8).
3. He executes justice for them in the courtroom of life, taking interest in every aspect of the trial (see Deuteronomy 10:18).
4. He shows particular favor to those who need it most (see Deuteronomy 7:7).

God is Judge. He loves the weak and vulnerable and sees to it ultimately that they receive justice. Scripture teaches this clearly. Yet many people who suffer from the pain and grief of broken relationships still find themselves facing hard questions. Why were their loved ones taken away? Why do they have to suffer so in this courtroom of accusation and misunderstanding? Why do they have to deal with so much pain and loneliness? Ultimately it is a question of why God allows pain.

Why Did God Let It Happen?

The death of a spouse or parent often leaves the family feeling betrayed by God. The same goes for divorcees. After all, they reason, He could have prevented it.

Trying to vindicate God in such situations is not always easy or even beneficial. It is possible to have unanswered questions and still come to know and trust God as One who is just, even though it may be the most difficult thing a person has ever done. What is more, God can handle our pouring our hearts out to Him, expressing the fear and anger that we feel.

Look, then, at three facts of human life.

1. This world is ruled by the prince of the power of the air (see Ephesians 2:2). Satan is both cruel and merciless. His primary vendetta is against God and he will do anything to get at Him, particularly hurting and destroying the crown and joy of God's creation, human beings.
2. We live in a fallen world. Unfortunately, knowledge of the fact that God is able to intervene in our fallen world where He is invited has caused many to feel condemned about their misfortune, perceiving that it was caused by their lack of faith. I believe, however, that the story of the man born blind (see John 9:1–5) indicates that much human disaster and tragedy is actually a result of corporate sin.
3. God's wisdom is beyond our own human comprehension. Earth is the center of a cosmic spiri-

tual battle between good and evil. God's ways are mysterious: Even in apparent defeat He is able to obtain victory. The death of Jesus on the cross is a perfect example of this. The Bible even says that in the last days God will allow the saints to be overcome (see Revelation 13:7). Many will triumph over the enemy of death by facing it head on, confident of their standing before a righteous Judge.

We may not understand why some people die. Whether we understand it or not, God's desire is to use widows and orphans to awaken our apathetic societies to the reality of the cosmic battle that is all around us.

For the victims of divorce the issues here are quite different. God can work miracles, but the one area He will not overthrow is the human will. He has created us to be volitional beings. This opens us to the potential to be loved, but it also opens us to the potential to be hurt and devastated by another's decisions. Love involves choice. If you are a woman in a secure marriage you know you are loved because your husband chose you above every other woman he knew. He retains the potential to love any other woman he encounters in his daily life, but he continues to keep choosing you. If there were no other women around, you could question the genuineness of his love because there would be nothing to test it.

Likewise, a father loves his child by making a choice to do so. He can actively or passively choose to divorce himself from that which is natural and right. His choice to leave is severely damaging for children because of the intensity of the relationship. In fact, we might even say that, for a young child, his father represents God. Because a child is completely dependent on his father, the loss feels like ultimate abandonment. A father gives a family identity and security. When he leaves by choice, it causes a crisis of identity. Who am I? Do I count? Am

I loved? We know intellectually that the only place of ultimate abandonment is hell—eternal separation from God—but many people feel as though they are living in hell on earth.

A woman may have been treated unjustly by her husband or children by their father but no one is ever treated unjustly by God. Still, many widows and father-less children feel betrayed by God at a time when they most need to know that He is there for them. Why?

A Question of Perception

As humans our perception is limited. What we experience most closely and most intimately becomes the basis on which we view all else. It becomes the lens through which we see the whole of life. As humans we have a keen perception of the natural realm and a hazy perception of the spirit realm. The spirit-to-spirit bond a wife and husband experience is largely due to the physical presence of the other; when one dies, that bond is torn. Because the surviving spouse perceives the reality of this natural realm more easily, he or she projects it onto God. In other words, we relate to each other in the natural realm, whereas relationship to God is in the spirit realm. Because the natural realm is so much clearer to us, we project what we learn in this realm onto our relationship with God.

This is, of course, a false perception, as God will never abandon us—or fail to provide for us or forget us. When a person's perceptions of God are skewed, the reason can usually be traced to his or her formative years. It is an amazing reality that our perceptions of God are influenced most cogently by our relationships with our parents, particularly our fathers.

Thus, in dealing with feelings of being betrayed by God, the most important question to ask is, What perception does this person have of his or her natural father? If his father was not there emotionally, most likely he will feel as though God is not there when he is overwhelmed emotionally. If her father died, she may feel abandoned by God. If his father was not a good provider, he will probably feel as though God never has enough for him. If she never had the right or privilege to express her heart, she is apt to feel condemned to silence before God.

The list could go on and on. These roadblocks need to be removed. They have been constructed by the individuals' choices to judge those who have hurt them; they can be broken down by forgiving, thus allowing God's blessing to flow. Refusing to show mercy means being cut off from God's mercy. Removing these roadblocks is the quickest way to receive the comfort, blessing, nurture and care we all need from a God who wants to lavish His love upon us.

Many times it is hard to identify abandonment by parents (particularly if they were good parents) because it happened in subtler, less obvious ways. Yet it is true that in any area of their hearts in which they could not give themselves fully to their children, those children have experienced abandonment. Recognizing and removing the resultant roadblocks of unforgiveness, resentment, bitterness, hurt, etc., allow for a clearer picture, a truer perception of God. "Blessed are the pure in heart, for they shall see God" (Matthew 5:8). That is when victims will see how God stands for them in every aspect of the trial and testing they are going through.

God's heart is broken and torn when deaths occur in relationships. He has already written reports in defense of the hurting and delivered them. The accuser of the brethren who wants to cut off hope has already been defeated. God will continue to work on behalf of widows and the fatherless until justice is fully upheld. He will make them a living testimony by restoring what others said was beyond repair. In the end neither they nor anyone else will be able to deny that God is with them.

four

God's Model Society

Deuteronomy is the last of the five books of the Law. These five books form the foundation of the Old Testament writings. They are to the Old Testament what the words of Jesus are to the New, the foundation on which all that follows is laid. Jesus referred to these books often and quoted from Deuteronomy on a number of occasions.

Why is this book so important to our study? The nation of Israel was on the brink of entering the Promised Land to establish God's government, rule and order; she was, in fact, to model a perfect society to the rest of the world. The content of this book is, therefore, extremely practical. It is also comprehensive: It records, among other exhortations, the final address Moses gave to Israel before his death, offering a summation of forty years' experience with God. Knowing God's concern for widows and the fatherless, we should not be surprised to discover many instructions here for their welfare. In fact, references to widows and how they are to be treated are more extensive in this book of the Bible than any other.

We have been exploring one of these many references, Deuteronomy 10:18, which speaks of God's dealing with widows and the fatherless. This teaching is to be the foundation of *our* dealings with them as well, something borne out by the rest of Deuteronomy. Let's shift our emphasis, then, to see just what our response should be in a model society set forth by God for His people.

Bring in the Tithe

> "At the end of every third year you shall bring out the tithe of your produce of that year and store it up within your gates. And the Levite, because he has no portion nor inheritance with you, and the stranger and the fatherless and the widow who are within your gates, may come and eat and be satisfied, that the LORD your God may bless you in all the work of your hand which you do."
>
> Deuteronomy 14:28–29

Tithes were an important resource for supporting the Levites and those who were most needy. As the people obeyed, God promised in turn to "bless [them] in all the work of [their] hands." I believe that many individuals and churches today fail to receive God's blessing because they fail to bless those He tells us to bless. When God blesses someone, He does not do half a job with a half-hearted attitude. He loves to bless and does it lavishly.

Celebrate the Feasts

> "Sacrifice the Passover to the LORD your God, from the flock and the herd, in the place where the LORD chooses to put His name.

". . . Then you shall keep the Feast of Weeks to the LORD your God with the tribute of a freewill offering from your hand, which you shall give as the LORD your God blesses you. You shall rejoice before the LORD your God, you and your son and your daughter, your male servant and your female servant, the Levite who is within your gates, the stranger and the fatherless and the widow who are among you, at the place where the LORD your God chooses to make His name abide. And you shall remember that you were a slave in Egypt, and you shall be careful to observe these statutes.

"You shall observe the Feast of Tabernacles seven days, when you have gathered from your threshing floor and from your winepress. And you shall rejoice in your feast, you and your son and your daughter, your male servant and your female servant and the Levite, the stranger and the fatherless and the widow, who are within your gates. Seven days you shall keep a sacred feast to the LORD your God in the place which the LORD chooses, because the LORD your God will bless you in all your produce and in all the work of your hands, so that you surely rejoice.

"Three times a year all your males shall appear before the LORD your God in the place which He chooses: at the Feast of Unleavened Bread, at the Feast of Weeks, and at the Feast of Tabernacles; and they shall not appear before the LORD empty-handed. Every man shall give as he is able, according to the blessing of the LORD your God which He has given you."

Deuteronomy 16:2, 10–17

Three times a year the Israelites were to observe feasts at the Temple—the Feast of Unleavened Bread (or the Passover), the Feast of Weeks and the Feast of Tabernacles. Freewill offerings from their produce meant that the Levites and the poor could join in. Celebrations were an important part of God's order and He made sure there was ample provision.

Widows and the fatherless were to be included in the feasts appointed by God. At these feasts everyone was to rejoice and celebrate. Why would God require a destitute widow to celebrate? What did she and her children have to celebrate?

God hates pretense and denial. So was He being insensitive by commanding widows and the fatherless to celebrate? No. Widows and the fatherless were able to celebrate at the feasts because of the kindness shown to them in their time of need. God had made provision for them. The model society that God desires to establish on earth is one where widows and the fatherless can celebrate and rejoice because of the kindness shown to them in time of need. First their needs were met through the tithe. Second they were made to feel welcome in the feasts.

Yet there is a deeper message. I do not believe people can feel included in special events unless they know they are included in everyday life. To be included means to feel fully part of something, not just like an add-on. For a widow to celebrate from her heart meant she felt protected from isolation in her pain. She was supported through her difficulties by people gently and sensitively walking through the time of destitution with her, making her feel included, understood and accepted.

I believe the condition of widows and the fatherless was a reflection of the condition of that society. I wonder how well we measure up?

Help the Needy Regarding Their Work

"You shall not pervert justice due the stranger or the fatherless, nor take a widow's garment as a pledge. But you shall remember that you were a slave in Egypt, and the LORD your God redeemed you from there; therefore I command you to do this thing.

"When you reap your harvest in your field, and forget a sheaf in the field, you shall not go back to get it; it shall be for the stranger, the fatherless, and the widow, that the LORD your God may bless you in all the work of your hands. When you beat your olive trees, you shall not go over the boughs again; it shall be for the stranger, the fatherless, and the widow. When you gather the grapes of your vineyard, you shall not glean it afterward; it shall be for the stranger, the fatherless, and the widow. And you shall remember that you were a slave in the land of Egypt; therefore I command you to do this thing."

Deuteronomy 24:17–22

Widows were honored by being given something to do. They were dependent on other people's generosity but they still had to work. If people are left with nothing to do, they lose motivation and significance. Allowing widows to work in the field without being despised enabled them to get out among people and be part of society. They were able to feel productive as they worked to meet their needs.

Likewise today it is important for widows and the fatherless to be included in church life in a significant way. This does not mean menial or demeaning labors. It means doing things that develop them in their gifts and callings.

This passage of Scripture also promises God's blessing in all the works of our hands. It ends by alerting the Israelites to the reason God made the command, so that they would remember that they were slaves in Egypt. The Amplified Bible says "earnestly remember." God had mercy on them as slaves in Egypt, delivering and honoring them with the riches of the Egyptians. Now they were to honor God by delivering widows and the fatherless from the cruel slavery of abandonment, isolation and neglect. Do not forget that every one of us was once helpless in our sin and rebellion against God, but He had mercy on us and delivered us from eternal damnation.

Be Aware of the Penalty

"'Cursed is the one who perverts the justice due the stranger, the fatherless and widow.' And all the people shall say, 'Amen!'"

Deuteronomy 27:19

This is the last verse on this topic in the book of Deuteronomy. After listing numerous areas of social responsibility, Moses then declared that curses would befall those who ignored twelve particular laws. Mistreatment of widows was included among them. The word used here for *justice* is the same as that used in Deuteronomy 10:18. If we do not uphold justice for the widow by becoming an active advocate for her and her children, we will be considered as those who are accursed.

Be Set Apart

These passages from the Law given to Moses by God cover important aspects of life for the widow and fatherless: having financial needs met, sharing in times of celebration and finding self-respect through honest work, and being assured of justice. There is one more commandment that I want to point out.

"For you are a holy people to the LORD your God; the LORD your God has chosen you to be a people for Him-

self, a special treasure above all the peoples on the face
of the earth."

Deuteronomy 7:6

Israel was to be a people who were holy (set apart)
to the Lord. This means they were to become like Him.
Not only were they to imitate the outward behavior of
God to execute judgment on behalf of the needy, but
they were also to do it with the same heart, passion,
jealousy and feeling that He does.

If you consider our study thus far—God's compassion
for the relationally vulnerable and our command to be
like Him—I am sure you will agree that the posture
called for is one of radical repentance, humility and crying out to God until we, too, are of like heart. It becomes
clear as you consider God's words in Deuteronomy that
He allowed widows and the fatherless to be a test for
the rest of the people. I believe the same is true today.
I wonder how well we are doing? Most likely we will
have to keep taking this test until we pass. Anything less
means that we will have failed to grasp the good news
of the Gospel and the reality of redemption.

five

Two Champions: Job and Josiah

In living out the principles that lead to God's model society we are not left without credible examples. Two Old Testament champions for the cause of widows and the fatherless were Job and Josiah. Job was a wealthy patriarch who lived a devoutly principled life. Josiah was a king of Judah, the southern kingdom of Israel. The Bible records that he was even more righteous than his godly predecessor, King David. Job's and Josiah's lives leave a stunning legacy for those who choose to live in their stead.

The Example of Job

If we look for a model of how God wants us to treat widows and the fatherless, we would be hard pressed to find a better example than Job. The book of Job is frequently viewed as a textbook on understanding suffering. This perception is too limited. The specific reason Satan asked to afflict Job was because Job was blameless, upright and feared God (see Job 1:1, 8–11). Job's life was one of such devotion to God that it infuriated Satan. Satan wanted to prove to God that if He lifted His protection from Job, Job would curse God.

The amazing thing is that God consented. Why? God allowed Satan to have access to Job because He had a much higher purpose for this righteous man. In the process He would also prove to Satan that no matter what happened to Job, he would not curse God. God allowed Job to be tested because He had absolute confidence that Job's character would stand firm and resolute no matter what. God's plan was to test and strengthen Job, enabling him to be trusted with twice as much as before.

If God was so confident about Job, I believe we should find in him an extremely good example of godly living. Job stood up under extreme testing because of his godly character. The New Testament exhorts us to follow Job's example of perseverance and patience in the midst of suffering.

> My brethren, take the prophets, who spoke in the name of the Lord, as an example of suffering and patience. Indeed we count them blessed who endure. You have heard of the perseverance of Job and seen the end intended by the Lord—that the Lord is very compassionate and merciful.
>
> James 5:10–11

Job got this perseverance and patience by living daily in the fear of God before he was ever tested.

One of the main ways we can see the development of patience in Job's character is in his dealings with widows and the fatherless. Many people speak of Job in a way that I believe is dishonoring to who he really was. Job was someone who knew intimate friendship with God (see Job 29:4). He was a spiritual giant, someone of stature, a claim attested by the bold declaration of God Himself: "Have you considered My servant Job, that there is none like him on the earth?" (Job 1:8).

It was the misunderstanding of Job's suffering that hindered those who tried to help him. Their assessments were narrow-minded; they made the wrong judgment that Job's suffering was caused by his wickedness. They proceeded to make him out to be a most ungodly person. The only purpose they served was to make Job very desperate for God.

A main charge against his character—proof, if you will, of his wickedness—was his supposed treatment of widows and orphans. Look, for example, at the words of Eliphaz in Job 22:9: "You have sent widows away empty, and the strength of the fatherless was crushed." The word *empty* here means empty in every sense, making life void of meaning and without cause or purpose. The Hebrew for the second part of this verse says literally, "the arms of the fatherless you have broken," an apt description, by the way, of the powerlessness of a fatherless child. The truth is that Job did the exact opposite of these two things Eliphaz accused him of. In Job's example we see godly principles to follow.

He Came to Their Rescue

Here is Job's response to Eliphaz: "When I went out to the gate by the city . . . I delivered the poor who cried out, and the fatherless and the one who had no helper. The blessing of a perishing man came upon me" (Job 29:7, 12–13). Job came to the rescue of those who had no means to help themselves. A man of influence, he stood up for them in the city gate, the place where important decisions were made.

He explains further the special care he gave those who were defenseless and helpless. "I was eyes to the blind, and I was feet to the lame. I was a father to the poor, and I searched out the case that I did not know" (Job 29:15–16). To be eyes to the blind and feet to the lame often requires inconvenience and a lot of patience. To be a father is very time-consuming. Job also made sure he had thoroughly searched out each individual case—once again requiring a great expenditure of time getting to know the individuals and understand their situations. Job's execution of justice involved active participation. Verse 14 further depicts Job's execution of justice as one that was wholehearted: "I put on righteousness, and it clothed me; my justice was like a robe and a turban." We see reflected here God's own defense of widows and the fatherless.

He Made the Widow's Heart Sing

Perhaps the most dramatic imagery in this section of Job is that he "caused the widow's heart to sing for joy" (Job 29:13). Once again Job mirrors God's nature. The Bible is full of such imagery. It is as if He takes the neediest of all and makes them His personal assignments. God asks, "Is there anything too hard for Me? Is any life too broken or destitute to serve as a triumphant message of My grace?" I believe God, like many of us, likes to take on challenges. He has given Himself an assignment. A special assignment. One in which He takes particular interest.

To make the widow's heart sing for joy is no small thing. Only those who are courageous would attempt such a thing. Job was such a man. The Lion of the Tribe of Judah is calling forth those of like courage in this day. Could you be one of them? If so, I pray you hear the call.

He Restored Failing Eyes

Job continues his defense against the accusations of his friends concerning widows and the fatherless in chapter 31. He lists many sins in which he knows he has had no part. He is so confident of this he sums it up by inviting a curse from God if he has done any of the things he lists. Verses 16–17 and 22 form part of this list: "If I have kept the poor from their desire, or caused the eyes of the widow to fail, or eaten my morsel by myself, so that the fatherless may not eat of it . . . then let my arm fall from my shoulder."

To cause the eyes of the widow to fail is to fail to restore hope. Hope is a confident expectation of good. Matthew 6:22 says that "the lamp of the body is the eye." How many of us would take the time to look into the eyes of a widow or her children to discern if her spirit is alive and buoyant or if her zest for life has been snuffed out? To do such a thing would require us to overcome our fear of intimacy. It feels vulnerable to expose oneself to someone else's pain and abandonment even for a split second. What is more, if we plucked up enough courage to overcome our fear of intimacy, would we then overcome the inconvenience of helping such a one?

Job goes on to say, "From my youth I reared [the fatherless] as a father, and from my mother's womb I guided the widow" (Job 31:18). A most amazing verse! Then he adds:

> If I have seen anyone perish for lack of clothing, or any poor man without covering; if his heart has not blessed me, and if he was not warmed with the fleece of my sheep; if I have raised my hand against the fatherless,

when I saw I had help in the gate; then let my arm fall from my shoulder, let my arm be torn from the socket. For destruction from God is a terror to me, and because of His magnificence I cannot endure.

Job 31:19–23

Job could not lift his hand against the fatherless because of his fear of God. This fear of God must return to us in this day. Job's life is a message to an end-time generation called to follow his example, to bring righteousness and justice to the earth.

The Example of Josiah

Josiah was one of the last kings of Judah. This king stood for righteousness like few others. He went through the entire lands of Judah and Israel and completely destroyed every altar erected to other gods and killed the priests who administered them. He also removed and destroyed the idols that had been erected in the Temple as well as tearing down the quarters that had been built for male shrine prostitutes (see 2 Kings 23:7)! The wickedness of the people in Josiah's day was so great that many of the altars he destroyed had been used for sacrificing children to the god Molech (see 2 Kings 23:10).

A prophet of the Lord had prophesied that Josiah would destroy the altar at Bethel about three hundred years before the event:

"O altar, altar! Thus says the LORD: 'Behold, a child, Josiah by name, shall be born to the house of David; and on you he shall sacrifice the priests of the high places who burn incense on you, and men's bones shall be burned on you.'"

1 Kings 13:2

As soon as Josiah discovered this prophecy he wasted no time. In radical, no-compromise actions he went throughout the land completely destroying every trace of idolatry. He was so determined to fulfill the word of the Lord that he even removed the bones of the former priests of the above-mentioned altar from their tombs and had them completely destroyed (see 2 Kings 23:16).

A Prophetic Destiny

Josiah had a righteous cause. He had a prophetic destiny to fulfill and would let nothing stop him. I believe there is an entire generation arising like Josiah that is going to be gripped with the reality of the prophetic destiny they are called to fulfill. When Josiah realized that his destiny had been outlined specifically years before it happened, he realized the extreme importance of what God had called him to do. God is about to imprint such a realization on the hearts of the Josiahs of this generation.

God's Warning

It is important to note that Josiah was not only a great reformer in purging the land of idolatry but also in the cause of defending the poor and needy. God said to Josiah's son, Shallum, King of Judah:

"Thus says the LORD: 'Execute judgment and righteousness, and deliver the plundered out of the hand of the oppressor. Do no wrong and do no violence to the stranger, the fatherless, or the widow, nor shed innocent blood in this place. . . . Did not your father [Josiah] eat and drink, and do justice and righteousness? Then it was well with him. He judged the cause of the poor

and needy; then it was well. Was not this knowing Me?'
says the LORD."

Jeremiah 22:3, 15–16

If the king and the people of Judah would follow this instruction, then the nation would continue to exist with kings ruling on David's throne. Otherwise Jerusalem would become a ruin (see Jeremiah 22:1–5). The kings after Josiah did not heed this warning. Judah was taken captive and the people were exiled to a far land.

Their Righteous Cause

Job and Josiah stood as champions for the cause of widows and the fatherless. It is interesting to note that the book of Job is one of the earliest Old Testament books and that Josiah, one of the last kings of Judah, ruled close to the end of the Old Testament record. This particular emphasis on two individuals with a no-compromise stance toward the treatment of foreigners, widows and the fatherless should speak to us today. Where are the Jobs and Josiahs of this generation? Could you be one of them?

six

Please Protect Me

In the preceding chapters we have looked at the place of widows and the fatherless in Old Testament society. While we have studied the predominant Old Testament Scriptures, there are, of course, others that support our findings, particularly in the Psalms and the writings of the prophets. I encourage you to explore these Scriptures for yourself and see the fullness of God's heart for these hurting individuals.

Having examined the Old Testament record concerning widows and the fatherless, we turn now to the New Testament and recall how Jesus lived out these principles. As we saw in the opening pages of this book, Jesus taught both in word and in deed how to protect and restore fragile lives. In the next two chapters we will see how His apostles and the early Church continued His mission.

Widows and the fatherless can be vulnerable physically, emotionally, mentally, sexually or spiritually. We will look at two areas in this regard, coercion and defile-

ment. To be like Jesus we need to hear the plea that is
common for both a fatherless child trying to cope with
being picked on at school and an aging widow whose
failing health forces her to be dependent on others. That
plea is: "Please protect me."

Coercion

A widow is to be treated with respect as the admin-
istrator and overseer of her affairs and her property. It
is not the job of the church to take over in these areas,
but instead to assist, help and advise. It is fine for a
widow to allow someone to oversee a specified area, but
the ultimate decisions must rest with her. God does not
overthrow human will; neither should we. Many times
widows are coerced (forced into obedience) and made
to do things because it is to someone else's advantage. I
like the word *coerced* because it portrays the subtle and
manipulative manner in which control may happen.

Jesus clearly condemned such actions, particularly
with reference to spiritual leaders: "Woe to you, scribes
and Pharisees, hypocrites! For you devour widows'
houses, and for a pretense make long prayers. Therefore you will receive greater condemnation" (Matthew
23:14).

Being on your own with no one to look out for you
can be a frightening experience. It can make you vulnerable to those whose intent is to take advantage.
Because a widow is minus the strength of her husband
or weakened by old age and failing health, she is more
easily swayed from her convictions and beliefs. If this
happens repeatedly, she feels victimized and helpless to
stand for what she feels is right.

In ministering to a widow, it is important to realize
this, being careful to go the extra mile in hearing what

she is trying to say. If she has experienced many strong voices coming at her, she has probably learned that her opinion does not amount to much, and she may need considerable help just to voice her own opinions.

This is also the case with the fatherless. They feel victimized and lack the strength that should have been imparted by the presence of a functional father.

It is all too easy to intimidate these people. It is important to remember that God's command not to afflict includes being circumspect toward them. Remember, anyone who has been wounded by authority needs to be restored. They need authority that will look out for them, see them, hear them, enter into their worlds and impart strength to help them speak up when they feel downtrodden, misunderstood, unheard and abandoned. Anyone in leadership must maintain open dialogue with those under him or her to avoid misunderstanding. To be under a person in authority is to be in a position of vulnerability. That is why those under authority must be given honor and not be overlooked.

Defilement

Another way widows and the fatherless are devoured is through relationships that defile. Although we do not know much about Mary Magdalene's past, other than the fact that Jesus cast seven demons out of her, I believe that she was a victim of relational defilement. The fact that she was one of the "many women who followed Jesus from Galilee [to Jerusalem], ministering to Him" (Matthew 27:55) could suggest that she had no home or family that she was responsible to stay behind and care for. Her responsiveness to Jesus' compassion, her utter devotion to Him as a trustworthy authority figure, as well as her awareness that He was her Lord all seem as well to point in this direction.

John 20:11–18 records the account of how the resurrected Jesus appeared to Mary Magdalene. Why did Jesus appear first to Mary (see Mark 16:9)? Surely if He were to stop and comfort anyone it would be His own mother or perhaps Peter who, after betraying Him, had wept bitterly. I believe that the reason Jesus appeared to Mary Magdalene was because, more than anyone else in His close circle of followers, she had been abused and abandoned by men. Jesus, unlike any other man she had known, was the first to love her truly. His death must have been devastating to her.

I believe it was for this reason that He stopped to reassure and comfort her in her great pain and distress. John 20:17 records Jesus as saying to Mary, "Do not cling to Me, for I have not yet ascended to My Father." I believe this command was to inform Mary of a change in the dynamic of her relationship to Jesus. Until this point she had clung to Jesus in the natural. Now the relationship had changed. She would learn to relate and cling to Him in a spiritual relationship that would supercede what she had known in the natural.

For Mary, Jesus had undoubtedly been the source of much love and nurture. Perhaps because of her healing relationship with Him, she could now receive this kindness through other human relationships. Jesus went on to say, "Go to My brethren and say to them, 'I am ascending to My Father and your Father, and to My God and your God.'" From this command we can note three things of importance:

1. Mary heard this directly from the lips of Jesus. The disciples would hear it from Mary. This communicated to Mary that she was an important part of God's plan, not just an onlooker on the fringe of

the group. During a time of major transition and change she belonged, she fit in and she was not going to be abandoned—something every widow needs to know.

2. When Jesus wanted to send someone to comfort and inform His disciples in their distress, He sent Mary. Jesus honored Mary by choosing her to be His messenger.

3. Jesus gave two commands to Mary. Firstly, not to cling to Him anymore and, secondly, to go and give a message to His disciples. The Greek word *de* translated "but" connects these two commands. Jesus was informing Mary that the disciples, and consequently the Church, would now replace Him as the source of the love and nurture she needed from natural relationships, effectively diminishing any opportunity for Satan to lure her into any unhealthy relationships.

If the Church does not protect widows, divorcees, singles and the fatherless by nurturing them emotionally and physically, they are uncovered prey. Women without husbands and children without fathers are particularly needful of copious amounts of clean, affectionate touch. If we ignore them, where else can they find wholesome affection and nurture? Certainly many beat the odds and find refuge in God, but many also find themselves unwillingly sucked into the embraces of people who use and defile.

Think about it. Why is pornography such a big industry? Because millions of fatherless people are trying to fill the void of a father's love in their lives. This includes those multitudes who grew up in homes in which the father was present but never knew how to express his love to his children. It is tragic how many teenage girls are so desperate for touch that they are vulnerable to any perverse individual who offers to give it to them.

It is not only physical abuse that defiles, of course. Spiritual abuse is a grave and insidious area of defilement. Widows are particularly vulnerable to this, and the enemy knows it. They need the covering of the Church to protect them from attacks of the enemy coming from false prophets and deceptive leaders.

Transference is particularly important here. Because of a widow's vulnerability, she is often sought out and influenced by wounded people who have hidden agendas. Although women are usually intuitive, they can be unable to discern wisely when emotional trauma or confusion bombards them.

Often the problem for them is whom to trust. Take, for instance, the many decisions that have to be made regarding children. What is safe and what is not? It amazes me, for example, that parents trust their young people to youth leaders they do not know—something that no one can afford to do in today's world. I know people whose lives are completely messed up because they were sexually abused in Christian camps.

False prophetic ministry is all too ready to lure people's hearts through false hope. False hope is tempting because it offers a pathway that is less painful and requires less sacrifice than the way of the cross. Forgiveness is the way of the cross. Truth and transparency are the way of the cross. Anything that short-circuits the way of the cross offers false hope.

Becoming fearful and paranoid about such things is not the answer, of course. Discernment is. Exposure to true prophetic ministry enables a widow to detect and discern the false more clearly. It also ignites within her a passion and love for Jesus, who is the true testimony of prophecy: "For the testimony of Jesus is the spirit of prophecy" (Revelation 19:10).

The easiest way to detect false prophecy is to know the voice of the Shepherd. The best protection from falsity is to know truth. True prophetic ministry protects and nurtures those who are vulnerable. It will not use a person's woundedness or vulnerability for its own advantage.

The enemy knows that a husband and father has authority to protect his home. When that is absent, Satan takes full advantage of the situation. Many helpless victims are under horrible onslaughts of physical and spiritual abuse from the enemy. We must fight for them. It is no help to turn our backs, suggesting that people need "to get their act together and stop being a case." The enemy ravages and torments people, often dulling their judgment by hitting their minds with confusion. We must fight for them and stop coercion and defilement from encroaching on the house of God.

seven

Apostolic Order

Jesus, the very Word made flesh, exemplified the Old Testament model for treatment of widows and the fatherless. Our question now is: How did those principles and His example translate into New Testament Church life?

The Early Church

The answer is an astonishing one. With the arrival of the Holy Spirit on the day of Pentecost, the newly formed Church was catapulted into a lifestyle that fulfilled God's model society:

> And they continued steadfastly in the apostles' doctrine and fellowship, in the breaking of bread, and in prayers. Then fear came upon every soul, and many wonders and signs were done through the apostles. Now all who believed were together, and had all things in common,

and sold their possessions and goods, and divided them among all, as anyone had need.

So continuing daily with one accord in the temple, and breaking bread from house to house, they ate their food with gladness and simplicity of heart, praising God and having favor with all the people. And the Lord added to the church daily those who were being saved.

Acts 2:42–47

It was this community way of life that caused the world to sit up and take notice. Widows and the fatherless were embraced so wholeheartedly, and with such generosity, that its message turned many hearts to God.

Now the multitude of those who believed were of one heart and one soul; neither did anyone say that any of the things he possessed was his own, but they had all things in common. And with great power the apostles gave witness to the resurrection of the Lord Jesus. And great grace was upon them all. Nor was there anyone among them who lacked; for all who were possessors of lands or houses sold them, and brought the proceeds of the things that were sold, and laid them at the apostles' feet; and they distributed to each as anyone had need.

And Joses, who was also named Barnabas by the apostles (which is translated Son of Encouragement), a Levite of the country of Cyprus, having land, sold it, and brought the money and laid it at the apostles' feet.

Acts 4:32–37

There are many definitions about what constitutes true revival and what signs identify a true move of God. The arguments are many and varied. But one thing you can be sure of, when people start opening their wallets freely and without persuasion, you are having a move of God. I have heard it said that the most sensitive nerve

65

in the human body is the one that moves your hand from your side to your back pocket. The open display of generosity demonstrated by the early believers broke obstacles in the spirit realm, allowing them to live under an open heaven. This newly formed organism—the Church—thrived and flourished.

This new society was not without difficulties, however, as the Church learned to find her way. Problems did arise, and the first one recorded involves the treatment of widows.

Widows Neglected

Here is the account.

Now in those days, when the number of the disciples was multiplying, there arose a complaint against the Hebrews by the Hellenists, because their widows were neglected in the daily distribution. Then the twelve summoned the multitude of the disciples and said, "It is not desirable that we should leave the word of God and serve tables. Therefore, brethren, seek out from among you seven men of good reputation, full of the Holy Spirit and wisdom, whom we may appoint over this business; but we will give ourselves continually to prayer and to the ministry of the word."

And the saying pleased the whole multitude. And they chose Stephen, a man full of faith and the Holy Spirit, and Philip, Prochorus, Nicanor, Timon, Parmenas, and Nicolas, a proselyte from Antioch, whom they set before the apostles; and when they had prayed, they laid hands on them.

And the word of God spread, and the number of the disciples multiplied greatly in Jerusalem, and a great many of the priests were obedient to the faith.

Acts 6:1–7

The Hebrew widows were being provided for but the Greek widows were being overlooked. The apostles gave careful attention to this inequity and their response shows something of the stance of the early Church toward widows. Their strategy was to choose seven men who were of honorable reputation, full of the Holy Spirit and wisdom. In other words they chose the very best to deal with the care and provision of the widows among them. It is also interesting that the apostles did not consider this work to be an issue solely of the natural realm: They recognized it as a spiritual issue. These seven men needed an impartation of the Holy Spirit to conduct their business and, thus, were commissioned by the laying on of the apostles' hands.

The Heart of God

Note that while the apostles realized the importance of this issue, they acknowledged that it was not what they themselves were called to do. Instead they were to give themselves continually to prayer and the ministry of the Word. These men were devoted to discerning the heart of God and then teaching, discipling and witnessing to others as God directed them. They recognized the importance of the position they held as apostles in God's newly formed Church and with their God-given authority commissioned others for various other roles. Taking care of the poor and needy would have been a preeminent issue.

Their immediate attention to this problem is not surprising: God's heart for widows and the fatherless would have been abundantly clear to these apostles. Remember that when the apostles gave themselves "to the ministry of the word," their written text was the Old Testament. The New Testament was built on the foundation of the Old. Though they had the teachings of Jesus in their hearts, these Scriptures were the only Bible the early Church possessed. Perhaps one of the reasons for their success was their firm mooring to the foundations laid down in the Old Testament.

When the apostles ministered the Word, you can be sure that they understood about God's model society as described in the books of the Law. Then, with the coming of the Holy Spirit upon them, they had a greater revelation of God's heart regarding that society. Finally, they could draw extensively from the years they had spent together with Jesus. Jesus modeled the Law perfectly, and they had witnessed His dealings with widows. They could now use their own godly authority to fulfill God's commands for the poor and needy.

Godly Authority

I believe it is significant that, when it came to appointing disciples to sort out the dispute concerning the widows, men were chosen for the job and not women. Having no husbands to look out for them, the widows were in need of the protection and authority of godly men. This is a key point for our understanding of the plight of widows and the fatherless today—particularly when these individuals have known only abusive authority from men, something that happens all too often. Those who are vulnerable need to be protected—not controlled and dictated to, but protected.

God has an appointed chain of authority throughout the universe. This can be seen even in the Godhead. The Father, Son and Holy Spirit are all equally God, but there is a clear chain of authority, the Father having ultimate command. Likewise Jesus is head of the Church and it is He who appoints those who have authority in the Body. Ephesians 2:19–21 indicates that apostles and prophets are an integral part of this chain of authority:

You are no longer strangers and foreigners, but fellow citizens with the saints and members of the household of God, having been built on the foundation of the apostles and prophets, Jesus Christ Himself being the chief cornerstone, in whom the whole building, being joined together, grows into a holy temple in the Lord.

As part of the foundation, the apostles are placed next to Jesus, the chief cornerstone, in the building and support of the structure. Authority is a weight to be carried. To be an apostle is not to be at the top, but rather at the bottom helping support the whole building. Few have the character to stand in such a position.

Do you see the chain of command at work in the distribution of food to the widows who were being overlooked? Jesus, as the head of the Church, had appointed twelve apostles. The apostles appointed seven men to oversee the treatment of the widows. If the enemy were to attack one of those widows, it would command the attention of those in authority over her. One thing Satan works overtime to do is break down this chain of authority. I believe this arrangement so angered Satan that he chose Stephen—a man "full of faith and power, [who] did great wonders and signs among the people" (Acts 6:8)—as one of his main targets. Stephen, as you will recall, was accused by false witnesses and martyred by an angry mob.

Another incident illustrates this chain of command. Acts 19:14–16 records the story of seven sons of a Jewish high priest trying to cast a demon out of a man. They "took it upon themselves to call the name of the Lord Jesus" (verse 13), as they had heard Paul do. The demon answered, "Jesus I know, and Paul I know; but who are you?" The demon recognized Paul's authority as an apostle appointed by Jesus and knew that these men were not under the authority of either Jesus or Paul.

The men, therefore, had no covering or protection. They were overpowered by the man who had the evil spirit. God honors the chain of command and authority that He has established. The enemy usually enters where this chain has broken down.

We have a desperate need for apostolic fathers in our day. God is raising up and restoring this ministry to the Church. We must embrace it. These apostles are not self-appointed but God-appointed.

Apostolic Ministry

If the full apostolic message is to be restored in these days, it must be birthed out of nothing less than the heartbeat of almighty God. If this happens, it will result in a ministry that is profoundly effective, far-reaching in its scope, thorough in its application and revolutionary in its results. It will be a ministry that is unafraid to target those considered out of reach—the most needy, the most desperate and the most destitute. What is more, this ministry will have the power to change their lives completely. Apostolic ministry is ministry rooted and grounded in the power, revelation and understanding of the cross. It results in the strongholds of the enemy being penetrated and destroyed. If your heart bleeds for the multitudes of people stuck in the trenches of life, one of the best things you can do is to pray for the full restoration of apostolic ministry.

This is why I strongly encourage widows and the fatherless not to shy away from what Peter Wagner and others have recognized as newly emerging apostolic churches. Among other things these churches are characterized by being strong in prayer, faith and vision. If you have been abused and abandoned by authority, this may be a hard thing to do. The solution to abusive or non-existent authority, however, is not *no* authority, but *good* authority. Often when individuals come out of brokenness, they gravitate toward people who will comfort and nurture. This is important, but it is also important to be around people who will impart strength and build them up again.

True apostles are fathers. Paul told the Corinthians that they had many instructors, but not many fathers (see 1 Corinthians 4:15). He exhorted the Corinthians to follow him as a father. After mentioning the many afflictions he had been through, Paul added that as well as all these afflictions he daily carried a deep concern for all the churches (see 2 Corinthians 11:28). He was an apostolic father. Apostles are like the high priest who carried every tribe of Israel over his heart. This was represented by twelve stones on the priest's breastplate, each stone representing one of the twelve tribes. Or put another way, an apostolic father carries churches in his heart in much the same way a father does his children. This fathering spirit is then passed on to the churches under his care.

Because a father carries his children in his heart, he knows when something disturbs one of them and comes to the rescue. We all need this kind of protection, particularly widows and the fatherless. Weak and broken vessels need to be under the authority of apostles who can carry them like a father and who will also impart strength back into their spirits. They need to be encouraged not to run away from this very necessary protection over their lives or let any wounding they have received from authority stop them from getting what they most need.

It is also true, however, that this anointed covering is not always present in our churches. It is a cunning strategy of the enemy either to leave the pastor alone, sometimes giving him a false sense that all is well, or to involve the pastor in difficulties that keep him distracted from tending his flock. One of the most effective ways to do this is to make him too busy. Meanwhile those under his authority are being pummeled by the enemy. The pastor cannot understand what is wrong and may develop a critical attitude toward those who are receiving the full onslaught of Satan's attack. The reason the sheep are being attacked is that they do not have the covering and protection they need.

Pastors, you must rise up in the authority and strength in which God has called you to walk. Your congregation suffers when you do not. Your spiritual condition is most imperative to the life and health of your congregation. If the enemy knows you carry clout in the Spirit he will be more tentative about touching those under you. One of his main aims is to disconnect and isolate you from your congregation.

Explosive Results

Finally, let us note that once the dispute concerning the widows was resolved by the oversight of the seven, the result was that the Word of God spread and the Church experienced a great increase in new disciples, even from among the priests (see Acts 6:7).

After Stephen was martyred, the saints in Jerusalem were scattered throughout the Roman Empire. Philip, also one of the seven, eventually preached in Samaria and along the coast of Israel with very powerful effect. I believe that many from the ranks of the fatherless will arise like Stephen and Philip. Because these men ministered particularly to the widows, they understood God's heart for the underprivileged. In the same manner, the fatherless have great potential to understand God's heart.

This message, if it is heeded, will have far-reaching effects. It is time for true apostolic fathers to rise up and see to it that widows and the fatherless are provided for, protected, nurtured, planted and strengthened in the Lord. These widows and the fatherless will serve as a powerful testimony and witness to the Gospel and will form a significant part of the army raised by God to bring in the harvest.

eight

The Test
of Undefiled Religion

The Church was being persecuted. The disciples were fleeing to the far corners of the world. To help encourage and instruct these followers of Jesus, various letters were sent to them and the fledgling churches they were starting. It is in one of these letters that we find the most striking New Testament exhortation concerning widows and the fatherless. It is in the letter of James:

> He who looks into the perfect law of liberty and continues in it, and is not a forgetful hearer but a doer of the work, this one will be blessed in what he does.
> If anyone among you thinks he is religious, and does not bridle his tongue but deceives his own heart, this one's religion is useless. Pure and undefiled religion before God and the Father is this: to visit orphans and widows in their trouble, and to keep oneself unspotted from the world.
>
> James 1:25–27

James exhorts believers to be doers of the work and not hearers only. Along with bridling the tongue, which we will discuss in a moment, he mentions two specific actions that indicate someone is a doer of the work: visiting orphans and widows in their "distress" (NIV) and keeping oneself unspotted from the world.

Today we hear many messages on keeping unstained by the world. Most Christians agree that this is a message of primary importance. Less often, however, do we hear any exhortations concerning widows and the fatherless. This is amazing, considering that we probably have more widows and fatherless in our time in history than any other.

Christianity does not mean detachment. We are not to keep ourselves holy merely for the purpose of being "holier than thou." True holiness is touchable. We are to keep unstained by the world so that we can reach out and touch those who are in need. God makes us holy for a purpose. Holiness will cause us to penetrate men's hearts as well as our cities and nations with the reality of Christ. It is time we realized our God-ordained destiny to make an impact on society and the nations about us.

A Lifestyle for the Church

James, the brother of Jesus, was an apostolic leader, a pillar in the Church. With the possible exception of Galatians, his was the first book to be written in the New Testament. More than any other book, it encapsulates the teachings of the Jerusalem Church in its most formative years.

The words *visit* and *keep* in James 1:27 are both expressed in a continuous tense, meaning we are to keep on doing these things. In other words, they are to become a lifestyle for us. This indicates that helping orphans and widows was a regular practice in the early Church. Since James wrote to the Jews who had been scattered due to persecution, this message went out from Jerusalem and was preached from Europe to India.

James gives us a test for the alternative, a distinctive quality of useless or worthless religion: an unbridled tongue! What we do with our tongues can be a good indication of whether our religion is useless or not. How easy it is in our day, when there are so many broken relationships and broken lives, for us to become vehicles for the enemy by judging other people's circumstances! This makes our Christianity worthless. God calls us to be change agents. Do our words impart life or death?

Hard, critical and judgmental attitudes toward widows or the fatherless make them feel as though they are untouchable—like those in Bible times who had leprosy and were considered unclean. This completely unbiblical attitude actually indicates that the person who holds such attitudes has his own kind of uncleanness in God's eyes. Jesus speaks to this problem:

> "Judge not, that you be not judged. For with what judgment you judge, you will be judged; and with the measure you use, it will be measured back to you. And why do you look at the speck in your brother's eye, but do not consider the plank in your own eye? Or how can you say to your brother, 'Let me remove the speck out of your eye'; and look, a plank is in your own eye? Hypocrite! First remove the plank from your own eye, and then you will see clearly to remove the speck out of your brother's eye."
>
> Matthew 7:1–5

The Bible says first to take the four-by-four plank out of your own eye. It is comical to picture a person with a log in his eye trying to get close to someone he or she is trying to help. God is the defender of widows and the fatherless. When we judge them, it is He with whom we will ultimately have to contend.

We are to speak the truth in love when required, but love always builds constructively and never pulls down or tears apart. It is impossible to build trust with someone who has a critical tongue. Even if we never criticize someone directly, those who hear us criticizing others will wonder if we do the same to them behind their backs.

A critical tongue is a heart problem: "Out of the overflow of the heart the mouth speaks" (Matthew 12:34, NIV). We have to earn the right to speak into people's lives. Widows and the fatherless are very sensitive to critical tongues and critical hearts because they are common recipients of such words and attitudes. James goes on in chapter 3 to warn us of how destructive the tongue can be.

> For we all stumble in many things. If anyone does not stumble in word, he is a perfect man, able also to bridle the whole body. Indeed, we put bits in horses' mouths that they may obey us, and we turn their whole body. Look also at ships: although they are so large and are driven by fierce winds, they are turned by a very small rudder wherever the pilot desires. Even so the tongue is a little member and boasts great things.
>
> See how great a forest a little fire kindles! And the tongue is a fire, a world of iniquity. The tongue is so set among our members that it defiles the whole body, and sets on fire the course of nature; and it is set on fire by hell. For every kind of beast and bird, of reptile and creature of the sea, is tamed and has been tamed by mankind. But no man can tame the tongue. It is an unruly evil, full of deadly poison. With it we bless our God and Father, and with it we curse men, who have been made in the similitude of God. Out of the same

mouth proceed blessing and cursing. My brethren, these things ought not to be so.

James 3:2–10

Planks in Their Eyes

As I have mentioned, the disciples had the examples of Jesus to follow in their decisions for the Church. I want to mention one story here that shows beautifully how Jesus dealt with those who had planks in their eyes and critical spirits in their hearts. This is the story of the woman caught in the act of adultery.

> Then the scribes and Pharisees brought to Him a woman caught in adultery. And when they had set her in their midst, they said to Him, "Teacher, this woman was caught in adultery, in the very act. Now Moses, in the law, commanded us that such should be stoned. But what do you say?" This they said, testing Him, that they might have something of which to accuse Him. But Jesus stooped down and wrote on the ground with His finger, as though He did not hear.
>
> So when they continued asking Him, He raised Himself up and said to them, "He who is without sin among you, let him throw a stone at her first." And again He stooped down and wrote on the ground. Then those who heard it, being convicted by their conscience, went out one by one, beginning with the oldest even to the last. And Jesus was left alone, and the woman standing in the midst. When Jesus had raised Himself up and saw no one but the woman, He said to her, "Woman, where are those accusers of yours? Has no one condemned you?"
>
> She said, "No one, Lord."
>
> And Jesus said to her, "Neither do I condemn you; go and sin no more."

John 8:3–11

This scenario was a set-up by the scribes and Pharisees to try to trap Jesus, enabling them to be able to bring accusation against Him. This incident illustrates how easy it is to criticize—without considering the darkness of our own hearts.

Because these accusers felt so self-righteous, relying on the usual cultural response to sins such as adultery, they had no compassion in their hearts for a humiliated and terrified woman. "This woman deserves to be stoned according to the Law of Moses," they said. It is so easy to take what God says without considering the full implications.

Jesus confronted the Pharisees for doing this when He said, "Woe to you, scribes and Pharisees, hypocrites! For you pay tithe of mint and anise and cummin, and have neglected the weightier matters of the law: justice and mercy and faith" (Matthew 23:23). Perhaps we don't like to look deeper into the true meaning of Scripture because it convicts us, pins us to the spot and forces us to make changes.

It is interesting that Jesus didn't make an immediate response to the fate of this woman. Likewise we must be careful not to jump to instantaneous solutions, stamping our judgments and decrees on helpless victims. John 5:19 says Jesus only did what He saw the Father doing. I believe Jesus waited in order to know the response His Father would give to this situation. Because Jesus only did what He saw the Father doing, His response to any situation was based on the very nature of the Father, not only on what He said. How easy to take a person's words and then divorce them from who that person is. God is a Father. Why does He provide us with a set of rules? To protect us, not to put us into bondage. The words Jesus spoke to the lady not only convicted her of her sin but also restored her in her spirit. This woman was clearly caught in sin and the response Jesus gave didn't condemn, but rather restored hope. How easy it is as the people of God to condemn people for acts that *can't* clearly be defined as sin. For this reason it is imperative to judge only as we hear from God (see John 5:30). When we fairly judge a case, we must make sure we fully understand what it is like to be in the person's shoes. Thus Hebrews 4:15 says that "we do not have a High Priest who cannot sympathize with our weaknesses, but was in all points tempted as we are, yet without sin."

A Heart of Forgiveness

Before we look at specific words that are patently unhelpful but regularly applied to the situations of widows and the fatherless, let's take the matter to prayer. Let's ask God for forgiveness for the times that we have not followed the biblical injunctions to defend and protect these vulnerable individuals and for the times that we have been critical and judgmental.

Father, forgive me for those times in which my tongue has not been yielded to You. Show me the areas in my heart with which I need to deal. Help me to embrace pure and undefiled religion and set me free from worthless religion. Lord, I ask You to forgive me for my critical words and attitudes toward [name(s)]. Turn my criticism into intercession. Give me eyes that see as You see. Let me be Your hands and feet. And let Your words of life come from my lips. Amen.

Part 2

Platitudes That Don't Heal

---
nine

"Don't Worry—God Is Your Husband"

What could sound more consoling, more meaningful, more wonderful than to tell a lonely widow that God is her husband! Since this statement is based on Scripture, Christians feel solidly biblical about offering it. "For your Maker is your husband, the LORD of hosts is His name; and your Redeemer is the Holy One of Israel; He is called the God of the whole earth" (Isaiah 54:5). Sounds good, right?

No, generally wrong.

It is not automatically beneficial to quote this Scripture for a widow; it may, in fact, be upsetting to her. While it is true that for some this may be the very expression of comfort they need, for most it is a shallow platitude.

Indirectly it minimizes a widow's loss: "What is your problem, is God not enough?" This attitude effectively shuts her down and shames her for feeling grief and sadness. It may add to her confusion if she initially feels hurt and angry with God about her husband's death. Add to this the fact that within her spirit there may remain a God-given desire to be in covenant relationship with a man, and we can see the potentially destructive nature of ill-spoken words.

The Hidden Treasure of Relational Intimacy

When you lose something in life, you come to value and treasure it more than those who still have it. Often it may happen that in the very barrenness of widowhood, God births revelations of the true depth, intimacy and glory of what marriage relationships can be. This revelation coming after the death of a husband causes great grief because of what could have been if he had remained alive. So why would God give such a revelation? Quite possibly for the purpose of affirming her desire for a human husband—just the opposite of the intended consolation people offer in the platitude from Isaiah 54:5!

In other words, "God is your husband" is said to widows in an attitude that implies, "Don't be ungrateful! Isn't it good enough to have God?" This causes her to feel ashamed for wanting a mate, almost as though she is betraying God by having such a desire.

God created us to yearn for fellowship with Him, indeed, but also with other people. Even after Adam had known fellowship with God, he still yearned for a wife. It is not wrong and sinful to desire a spouse. God is the widow's husband but He also created her to have depth of fellowship and intimacy with fellow humans.

After the death of a spouse it is imperative for the remaining partner to allow an extended period of time to grieve and adjust to life without the loved one. It is also vital for such a one not to rush in to another marriage relationship without first giving it time to develop and mature as a friendship.

Even those whom God has specifically called to live a life of celibacy have relationships of depth. Paul the apostle was such a person. For the well-being of a future marriage, it is important to develop healthy relationships of depth in the present. For most this will take time. For some it will require overcoming emotional distances and fears of intimacy. For others it will mean learning to have emotional boundaries. Whatever the situation, developing relationships is an important part of fulfilling the callings God has on our lives.

Hannah's Calling

While a widow can learn to be content in her present circumstances, it can also be true that God has impregnated her with relational vision and destiny. When you are pregnant with something, you cannot ignore it and pretend it is not there. It has become part of you. This is a paradox with which many widows learn to live.

A good example of this is found in the life of Hannah who was barren and yearned deeply to bear children for her husband. In her desperation she cried out to God, who in the course of time caused her to conceive. Before this happened, however, her condition is described in 1 Samuel 1 with the following words: *provoked severely, miserable, wept and did not eat, grieved, bitterness of soul, wept in anguish, affliction, sorrowful spirit.* How long did this go on? Year after year, verse 7 says. When Hannah did conceive, she gave birth not just to a son, but to a prophet, Samuel. She had made a vow to God that if He allowed her to conceive, she would dedicate her child completely to His service.

One of the reasons Hannah was so deeply afflicted about her barrenness was because she had a God-given call and destiny to give birth to Samuel, the man who would one day anoint David as king. God waited until she was prepared to surrender the child completely to His service before He allowed her to conceive. Many times God withholds for a season because He has an ultimate plan much greater than we realize. Hannah's husband tried to comfort her with the fact that he loved her despite the fact that she was barren, but she would not be consoled. She had a husband who loved her but she could not be satisfied with that. God had put within the core of her being the desire to conceive and bear children.

Hannah's anguish caused her to cry out to God. By this her heart was prepared for God's ultimate purpose, giving birth to a prophet of Israel. Hannah did not realize the fullness of what was going on with her. She did not know the impact her heart's cry would have on the whole nation of Israel.

Are you a widow who faces such a longing? Then realize that you have a Husband who loves you so much that He died for you. This is a great source of comfort. But, like Hannah, you may find that this loving relationship does not lessen the desire to fulfill your God-given mandate. Part of that mandate could very well include marriage. If there is an inconsolable grief in your heart about not having a husband, it is likely because of one or both of two reasons:

1. You are looking for a husband to meet the needs in your heart that only God can meet.
2. Somewhere within the core of your spiritual being is an inner knowing that you are called to be married. It is part of your God-given destiny. Coupled with

this may be a God-given revelation of the full glory of what marriage is meant to be.

You can expect that others may not understand your anguish and may even judge you for it. Remember, God understands. Only He can meet the deepest longing of your heart. If that need is relational, He wants to become your primary source, no doubt using others to help bring you to that place. If the need has to do with fulfilling your God-given destiny, He will do the work necessary in your heart, bringing it to pass in His perfect timing, because just as with Hannah, He knows the end of the story from the beginning.

"Just Put Away the Past"

Those who have faced the devastation that comes from being fatherless are frequently encouraged to "put away the past" and move on. Rather than provide solace, however, these words actually block the way to freedom.

As we will see in this chapter, there are three primary reasons that those who grew up fatherless do not want to address issues from the past. The first is because they have a theological problem with it. They quote Scripture and feel justified in never looking back: "The apostle Paul said that we must forget those things that are behind," they argue.

The second reason actually skirts a scriptural admonition: They might be expected to forgive the one who hurt them.

The third reason is fear of facing painful memories. What if it hurts more than they can bear?

Let's look more closely at these issues and the misguided thinking behind them.

1. Didn't Paul Tell Us to Forget the Past?

Many people assume that the best way to be healed from hurts is to ignore them. This is not true. It cannot be true when the Spirit of Truth reveals and brings everything into the light. To ignore the past is to ignore reality, which is to ignore truth.

Still, they persist and quote Scripture as the basis for their decisions. They turn, in particular, to Philippians 3:13–14:

> Brethren, I do not count myself to have apprehended; but one thing I do, forgetting those things which are behind and reaching forward to those things which are ahead, I press toward the goal for the prize of the upward call of God in Christ Jesus.

True, Paul said he forgot those things that were behind. *Forget*, however, means "to deal with," not "to ignore." The only way to forget a festering wound from the past is to expose it to the light and heal the source through forgiveness.

When Paul said, "I forget that which is behind," he was talking about a process much more thorough than our twenty-first-century Christian minds have been led to believe. Remember that Paul championed the message of sanctification, which in layman's terms is the process of getting your heart sorted out (transformation). This happens through death and rebirth. The Adamic nature within us is to be killed, not merely patched up. It is by faith that we are first crucified with Christ and then resurrected into newness of life. This enables us to say with Paul, "It is no longer I who live, but Christ lives in me" (Galatians 2:20).

While it is true that according to 2 Corinthians 5:17 we are a new creation and old things have passed away, this reality still has to be worked out experientially. Our Adamic nature is a master of deceit and hides from the light. It tries to deceive us into believing that it has been slain, and then it tries continually to resurrect itself. That is why Paul said, "I die daily" (1 Corinthians 15:31).

Sanctification also includes touches of God's love that bring healing and restoration to areas of wounding within the human spirit. (This can be seen in Ephesians 5:25–29 in the words *washing, nurture, cherish* and *cleanse*. The word *cleansed* used here is the same Greek word that is used in 2 Corinthians 7:1, referring to cleansing of defiled flesh and spirit.) In the Tabernacle of Moses the bronze altar speaks of death and resurrection, the laver of the washing with water by the word.

Past Wounding, Present Reality

Paul was well aware that wounds from the past can live on in the present. Past wounding that remains unaddressed is indeed a very present reality.

We often recognize this on a large scale: We see how wounds between people groups or even nations can live on for generations. In order to bring healing to these warring factions, it is necessary for the descendants to confess to each other the sins of their fathers, a process known as identificational repentance. Although the ongoing nature of hurt from the past is recognizable on a national level, however, many fail to see and acknowledge it on a personal level. Thus, grieving and hurting individuals are told to move on from the issues that caused them pain.

If you have never dealt with childhood wounding in your spirit, then it is very much at issue in the present. Paul said in 1 Corinthians 13:11:

When I was a child, I spoke as a child, I understood as
a child, I thought as a child; but when I became a man,
I put away childish things.

Childish ways of behaving and thinking are to be "put
away," but once again this is a much more involved
process than merely forgetting. If childish things are not
put away, we become children in adults' bodies. To put
it another way, although we are adults, we still behave
in childish ways because we have not dealt with childhood wounding. The only way to receive healing is to
go to the root of the problem.

The deepest and most powerful roots in our hearts are
those that originate in childhood. During our formative
years, the foundations are laid for all the ways we react,
behave, perceive and think. Formative events are usually
long forgotten, but they still control the way we live in
the present. Letting God reveal and expose hurtful events
seems to cause earthquakes in our hearts, because they
shake the very foundations upon which we have built.
Often, though, He wants us to build new foundations.

By the death of Jesus on the cross all our old fleshly ways
of behaving can be brought to death. By the power of His
resurrection new foundations can be laid. It is by faith in
the death and resurrection of Jesus that this process can
take place. The work that Jesus did through the cross is
finished (see John 19:30). It is final and complete. But we
need to appropriate that which has already been done for
us. Remember that sanctification is a process by which we
must continually surrender our hearts to God and exercise
faith in the power and working of the cross.

Past Mistakes and Victories

Even if we address issues from the past and find healing in Christ, we are not through. We have to remain

91

alert. After past issues have been resolved, the enemy still uses our mistakes and victories to hold us back.

Paul knew this well, as before his conversion he had zealously persecuted Christians with hopes of destroying the Church. Paul let God do a deep work of sanctification in his heart once he was saved. This involved dealing with the roots of anger, bitterness, resentment and unforgiveness that had caused him to oppose the Christian faith so strongly.

We have all made mistakes in the past. When we ask for forgiveness, we are forgiven straight away. It is then that we can let God reveal, expose and crucify the roots that caused us to err in the first place. Even after this has happened, our enemy still tries to use the past to bring condemnation. Satan is, after all, the accuser of the brethren. He hopes to use the past to render believers ineffective.

If these past mistakes have been forgiven, however, and the causes dealt with at a deep root level, then Paul says he can forget (see Philippians 3:13). Instead of hindering him, his roots now become a testimony to the mercy and grace of God. The grace of God is that which imparts strength to overcome personal weaknesses.

It is not only our mistakes that can keep us tied to the past but also our successes and victories. If we let the good things we have achieved in the past become our measures of success, we will become prideful and possibly apathetic about pursuing a deeper, more intimate relationship with God in the present. Surprisingly, even focusing too much on the things we plan to accomplish in the future can prevent us from pressing on to know Christ. All things, not only the past, need to be brought into the light.

Thus, as the fatherless deal with the hurts that have affected their lives, they need to remember three principles we glean from Scripture:

1. We must not ignore issues from the past; we must first overcome them before we can forget them.
2. Any wounding from the past that has not been addressed is still very much in the present.
3. Even after we have crucified or overcome the past, the enemy still tries to use our mistakes and even our victories to keep us from the love and grace of God.

2. Victims and Forgiveness

A second reason people do not want to look back with a desire to heal the past is because they prefer to live in self-pity and victimization. Victims of the past who choose not to seek healing tend to fall into two categories:

1. Those, as we saw above, who ignore the past and refuse to face it.
2. Those who prefer to wallow in self-pity and nurse their wounds.

The people in this second category are choosing not to forgive whoever has hurt them—even if the hurt was unintentional. It is not unusual for a child to face issues of forgiveness toward a parent who "left him" by dying. The same can be true of a widow who feels abandoned by her spouse. For those who do not want to forgive, the past may then be used to justify their pitiable state.

Forcing someone to speak words of forgiveness, by the way, is a useless exercise. I have known fatherless teen-agers who were pressed into expressing "forgiveness," but it was only a ritual with little significance—except perhaps to cement the already existing anger. Feelings reveal the heart. Until a person is truly ready to walk the path of forgiveness, little real healing will take place.

It helps if we understand that forgiveness is a process rather than a one-time act. It is like throwing a yo-yo down again and again until, finally, the string breaks and the yo-yo rolls away. Beginning that process by speaking words of forgiveness to the best of one's ability and continuing, with God's help, to walk in His light can result in a changed and healed heart. In fact, unless a person comes to feel genuine love for the one who hurt him, then I do not believe that forgiveness has been fully accomplished.

It is not unusual, after praying a prayer of forgiveness, for all the hurt, anger and pain in a person's heart to erupt once more. That is why we must confirm again and again, with God's help, that we have chosen to forgive. In fact we soon realize that we cannot do it without God's help. If we remember other hurts, then we must express forgiveness for those as well. Remember that Jesus said the number of times we are to forgive is seventy times seven (in other words as many times as necessary).

Are you one who uses self-pity as a crutch? Do not let self-pity stop you from uncovering the root causes in your heart and letting forgiveness and sanctification bring full restoration. It is not easy to feel the pain of remembrance, but once we face it with the desire to forgive, then we are able to surrender it to God fully and break the bondage of self-pity.

3. Fear and the Past

Fear is the third major reason that prevents people from facing their pasts. The things we have buried can be so painful that we are frightened to look at them in case they overwhelm us and we can no longer cope. That is why we can only face these things by firmly grasping the hand of Jesus and trusting Him to be there for us as a refuge. He is gentle and kind and does not give more than a person can handle. He often brings up remembrances only after a person has been walking with Him for some time and has grown enough in faith to have the strength and security in His love to face them.

People might also have fear about looking at the issues of their lives lest they become too self-absorbed. There is so much work to do for the Kingdom, they reason. Surely it is best to put away one's past and get on with the work of reaching the lost.

Let me add this: It is true that some evangelists, whose main focus is getting people saved, have leveled charges of "navel-gazing" against the prophetic ministry. In truth, however, these two ministries need to work side by side, first bringing in the fish and then cleaning them. Every area of a person's heart that is healed and restored is an area in which that person has authority to bring restoration both to the saved and the unsaved. A sanctified and restored church is a church moving in such power, authority and love that the unsaved flock to Jesus.

The High Call

In dealing with the past it is often best to receive the help of a counselor. It is important, however, to find a counselor who deals with root issues through the power of the cross. Many counselors only deal with past issues on a surface level. This is like chopping branches off a tree instead of going to the root. If healing is to take place, the ax needs to go to the root (see Matthew 3:10). Temporary solutions might seem easier in the short term, but problems will recur.

Have you chosen to face your past, rather than "just put it away"? Remember that at all times in every stage of the healing process, you must press toward the high call, which involves pursuing Jesus with unrelenting vigor. The prize of this upward call is deep and intimate fellowship with God. Nothing could be more wonderful. This call is so glorious that everything else, including the past, pales into insignificance.

If you would proceed higher, you also must go deeper. The higher the building, the deeper the foundations have to be laid, and the stronger they must be. Those who are aware of the height of the calling we have in Christ are the very ones who will be most diligent about exposing the shaky and unstable foundations of their lives to Him. This process must continue until everything we do, everything we say and everything we are is a reflection of Christ in us.

To forget the past is to expose it to Christ so that it no longer has power over us. It is not an easy process but the pain of it is nothing when our eyes are full of the glory of the One we are pursuing.

eleven

"Try to Be Like Hosea"

My husband has just left.
What do I do?
My world is falling apart.
I tried my best to stop it from happening
but . . .
*   but . . .*
then he was gone.
Someone said I have to be like Hosea and stand for
my marriage, so I read the book of Hosea in the Old
Testament.
If I have to be like Hosea, I have to keep loving my husband
even though he's sleeping with another woman!
God, I don't know if I can do that, but I'll try—I'll try
anything.
If only I could measure up to Hosea, then my husband
would come back to me.

We turn in this chapter to the plight of the person whose
spouse has left. There is much teaching exhorting those
who are facing divorce to follow the example of Hosea.

Some of this teaching is good teaching and it is not my purpose to refute it. My concern is that many times individuals are expected to measure up to an impossible ideal. The result is often demeaning and soul-destroying for the person left behind. Our purpose for those in the midst of traumatic experiences should be to restore, not to add further wounding to an already shattered life.

Let's look at the story of Hosea and its meaning for any individual in a broken marriage. As I noted earlier, women may face this circumstance more often, but many men have been on the losing end as well.

The Story and the Message

Hosea was a prophet to the nation of Israel between 800 and 700 B.C. Israel had broken her covenant with God by following after idols. In the midst of this debauched nation lived Hosea, a man who heard and obeyed God's voice. When God told him to marry a woman who was a known adulteress, he obeyed. His marriage to Gomer was understood to be a symbol of God's relationship with Israel, and he loved her just as God loved His rebellious people.

Gomer bore Hosea three children and each child's name was a prophetic word to the nation of Israel. Hosea's message was one of repentance. Even though the Israelites had turned from God, He was still prepared to be their God if they returned to Him. There is some speculation that the last two children that Gomer bore were not Hosea's children. Of the first child the Bible says that Gomer "bore him a son." Concerning the second and third children it reads "bore a daughter" and "bore a son." After this Gomer left Hosea to pursue her life of adultery and prostitution.

Then said the Lord to me, Go again, love [the same] woman [Gomer] who is beloved of a paramour and is an adulteress, even as the Lord loves the children of Israel, though they turn to other gods and love cakes of raisins [used in the sacrificial feasts in idol worship]. So I bought her for fifteen pieces of silver and a homer and a half of barley [the price of a slave]. And I said to her, You shall be [betrothed] to me for many days; you shall not play the harlot and you shall not belong to another man. So will I also be to you [until you have proved your loyalty to me and our marital relations may be resumed].

Hosea 3:1–3, AMP

What Is God Saying?

God told Hosea not only to marry Gomer but also to take her back after she had lived a life of blatant adultery. The reason God told him to do this was because Hosea, being a prophet, was to symbolize the message God had given him to preach. Does God always tell people to do this? No.

If a woman is told to perform like Hosea, she faces a number of problems. First, it puts her in a performance trap. Now the whole future of her relationship with her departing or departed husband is dependent on how well she performs. How is a woman in this situation going to measure up to a prophet commissioned by the Lord? She may try but will likely end up feeling utterly condemned.

To Love Unconditionally

A second problem is that it puts her in the position of having to woo her husband. This effectively reverses what is considered the normal order of a man wooing a woman. We see this concept most perfectly in the fact that as the Bride of Christ we have been drawn first by Jesus' love. "We love Him because He first loved us" (1 John 4:19).

For a woman to have to woo her husband increases her pain by pointing out the reality that he once wooed her but has now abandoned her. It is also likely that she never was properly courted by her husband. The wounding from this reality within a woman's heart is great. Now she is expected to act toward him as he should have acted toward her.

I believe it is wrong to put such an expectation on a woman. It is not possible for her to do this without seriously impairing her self-worth. Am I saying not to love her husband unconditionally? No. Jesus asks us to love unconditionally. I am saying not to expect her to measure up to a behavior that is often impossible to achieve.

Showing Jesus' unconditional love for a departing husband *can* woo him back to the one he first loved, but there is no guarantee. Everyone has free will. Ultimately all choose which paths they take. Decisions cannot be made for them. Jesus, by dying on the cross, showed unconditional love for the whole human race. Some choose to follow Him; some choose not to. These women facing separation and divorce need to see that their identities are not determined by whether or not their husbands return. Some husbands' returns are due as much to their own selfish needs as to the unconditional love shown by their wives.

The Conditions

A third problem for a woman who tries to be like Hosea involves the conditions under which Hosea received Gomer back. God's love is unconditional. No matter what we do, He still loves us. This does not mean that He does not have conditions, only that His love for us is not determined by meeting the conditions.

To love unconditionally does not mean to receive a wayward spouse back under any circumstances or conditions. When God told Hosea to pursue Gomer again, she had come to the absolute end of herself, suffering the effects of her sin. She was being sold in the market as a slave. What a pitiable sight she must have been! When Hosea redeemed her, he gave her a set time to prove that she had turned from her adulterous ways and would be loyal to him. A period of time was necessary to reestablish and restore broken trust. God's condition on retrieving Israel as a covenant people was for her to turn from idols and worship Him alone.

Under no circumstances are individuals to be received back until they show fruits of repentance. They must be made accountable for what they have done. Remorse must not be confused with repentance.

That is why it is important to wait until the fruits of a changed heart are clearly seen. If a woman's husband is having an affair with another woman, it is not love to allow him to return to her unless there is true repentance. If she allows him to return with no conditions, she is likely to end up more abused than previously. It is not love to become a doormat someone can walk all over. Love lays down its life for a person by processing the hurt through the power of the cross, but it also confronts with truth what the person has done.

Anyone confronting an adulterous spouse must make sure he or she has dealt with his or her own hidden animosity through the cross. "Brethren, if a man is overtaken in any trespass, you who are spiritual restore such a one in a spirit of gentleness, considering yourself lest you also be tempted" (Galatians 6:1). Gentle but holding to account. If the abandoned person's behavior

101

contributed to the separation, it needs to be confessed with a humble and repentant spirit. It is both sinful and destructive to face a situation like this with vindictive motives or with the intent of gaining ammunition in order to repay the hurt.

The word *restore* here is a command. To restore does not mean "cover over." Many attempt to avoid conflict by pretending that hurts never happened. That is why marriages in which couples argue in order to share their wounded feelings actually have good potential to reach resolution. They are more likely to understand and love one another. If hurts are deliberately ignored in order to avoid conflict, the marriage partners will have a harder time restoring fellowship.

Even when we lose it and say things we should not have said, God still asks us to hang in there and pursue the process of restoration. A mediator or counselor may be needed whenever it becomes obvious that injured parties are not able to process their thoughts and feelings constructively.

Let Go or Hang On?

When there is an ongoing sexual relationship outside the marriage, reconciliation is nearly impossible. There is, however, a difference between someone who slips in a moment of weakness and repents and someone who has decided to enter into a new relationship. Many women live in the hope of their relationships being restored, even after they are clearly finished. There comes a point when this has to be acknowledged. Women are often exhorted to hang on when it would be more helpful for them to be exhorted to let go.

I have heard of situations where women have stood, believing against the odds, and the miraculous has happened. God cannot make a husband return. He will not overthrow free will. God does, however, in His fore-knowledge see when a husband will return. In such situations I can well believe that God could grant the woman the strength to believe Him for this. Unfortunately the number of women left "hanging on" and never having their hopes realized far exceeds those who experience the miraculous.

Abusive Relationships

The Hosea platitude is oftentimes used to instruct married couples to stay together even if the relationship is abusive. This is dangerous advice. In the Old Testament many abusive behaviors were punished by death. *If someone is in a relationship in which he or she is exposed to sexual rage, habitual physical violence or extreme emotional abuse, or if the partner is in an adulterous relationship or children are at risk of being sexually, physically or emotionally abused, it is necessary to separate from the abusive partner.*

This is not to suggest divorce, but it is imperative for the person's sake and for the sake of the children to separate. Matthew 18:15–20 implies that the church will stand with a person who has been sinned against. If the abuser is a Christian and the outlined procedure has been followed, the church will hold that one accountable. In dealing with abusive situations it is important to realize the following:

1. Many people in such a situation feel powerless to do anything. This is particularly true if they grew up in alcoholic, addictive or abusive homes. Powerlessness is a learned behavior and perception. If this is the case the person needs to be encouraged

and shown that he or she is not, in fact, powerless and can separate from the abusive situation.

2. Many women continue in abusive relationships for years because of wrong understandings of love. False definitions of love say that one must protect and hide perpetrators in their shameful and sinful ways. To tell these women to be like Hosea may cause them to continue in their wrong and destructive patterns of love. "If only I try hard enough I can keep this family together." This way of thinking originates in a childhood in which the child believes the conflict within the home is her fault. Children naturally feel this way. It causes them to try to perform harder and harder in order to fix the unpleasant environments in which they live.

3. Addictive homes teach children that there is no point in challenging something that is not right. To do this would result in unmerciful retribution. To be able to separate requires that such intimidating fears be overcome. This is not an easy thing as this level of fear often causes people to feel completely paralyzed. More than anything else, a woman needs friends who will stand with her and by her.

4. Fear of not being able to survive financially and of losing valuable assets such as car and home stops many from separating. "How can I go it alone?" But that is small loss compared to living in a soul-destroying situation. Pray for the person to be able to see this, to have the strength to act and to see the solutions and resources that are there.

If there is a need for a protection order, get one. Reconciliation can only happen once the person practicing abusive behavior has responded to professional counseling and has been truly changed and transformed in his or her behavior. This will take time, first to receive extensive counsel in order to address the root issues and then to demonstrate continually the fruits of repentance.

Those who have been in abusive relationships and are now divorced need to make sure that they have received full and proper counseling and ministry in order to prevent identical patterns from happening again.

The Outcome

God's heart's desire was to restore His relationship with the nation of Israel. History shows us this did not happen in Hosea's time, but God has not given up. Hosea prophesied that this relationship will, in fact, be fully restored before the end.

Presumably Hosea was able to live with Gomer for the rest of his life. Perhaps you are a divorcee hoping that this, too, will be the end of your story. This may or may not happen, but as you are able to turn from your own efforts to measure up you will be able to focus more clearly on God's love for you. Although divorce breaks the marriage covenant, God is still able to restore divorcees to be covenant brothers and sisters in Christ. While this may take years to become reality, God never gives up on anyone or any situation. In heaven you may rejoice to see how your faithful prayers for the one who hurt you have, in fact, brought that one to repentance.

God loves you more than you will ever know. Perhaps you can begin to pray now:

God, whether my husband comes back or not, I surrender to You. I commit him to You, Lord, and ask you to draw him to You.

God, it feels as though one of my limbs has been chopped off. I don't know how to survive. Inside I am screaming with pain and paralyzed with fear. How can I live without him?

God, I need You as never before. I know I can't measure up to this Hosea thing—I just haven't got it. But I determine to focus on Your love for me because I know I can only love as I am first loved.

Part 3

Ministry Nuts and Bolts

twelve

Can I Trust You?

Widows and the fatherless face again and again questions of trust. To lose a friend is one thing, but to lose a husband or parent cuts to the core of a person's being. Those who experience divorce are particularly afraid to trust anyone at all. After divorce or the death of a parent or spouse, there is often a great fear to open up and trust in case the relationship is once again cut short.

How are we to minister to those who have faced such significant losses? What is our part in the process of restoring trust? Let's begin with a look at ministry itself.

The Work of Ministry

Most people experience distress of some degree in their lives. Add to this the fact that many people in the local church—not to mention those outside the church— have huge gaps in their most basic developmental needs and we get an idea of the enormous challenge. How can we possibly meet this huge demand?

Let's begin our exploration with this premise about ministry: The five-fold ministry of apostles, prophets, evangelists, pastors and teachers listed in Ephesians 4:11 is for the purpose of "the equipping of the saints for the work of ministry" (verse 12). In other words, church leaders are not supposed to do all of the ministry. Rather, they are to equip the rest of the Body to do it. The Body, thus called and equipped, can then minister to a variety and great quantity of needs. Our lack of understanding and implementation of this fact has cost us dearly, as many of those who have come to our churches with needs have slipped through our hands because we are not ministering and caring for them.

This is particularly true of ministry to widows and the fatherless. We live in a fast-paced world where performance is often lifted above principle and integrity. We simply do not have time. We figure that widows and the fatherless do not have much to contribute to the progressive growth plan of the church. Their contributions are often viewed as minimal. This mindset is, of course, far from the truth.

Understanding, then, that we are called to ministry and that our ministry can help widows and the fatherless fulfill their own callings, we move to the next question.

Are We to Minister to Everyone?

God says we are to defend widows and the fatherless. Helping someone who wants to heal and grow is a mandate for us as part of the Body of Christ.

But what about the person who does not want to take responsibility for his or her life and begin putting the

110

pieces back together? The person who, for instance, uses a victim mentality to achieve her goals? Is God asking us to pour out our lives for a person who is not prepared to change?

Many in the church become skeptical when some, because of unhealed wounds, act like leeches on the Body of Christ. In fact, one of the enemy's strategies to make churches ineffective is to tie them up ministering to people who want their needs met but will not face the changes they have to make. They want to be pampered.

Compassion and mercy do not pamper. They heal and restore. A simple analogy is the patient who wants to tell her doctor continually about her sickness, but who will not accept the surgery that could cure it. Compassion and mercy say, "I see your misery. I identify with it and will comfort you, but I have a determination to see you whole, even if the process may become painful."

Oftentimes a person who is sincere about growing and changing does not receive any help because the one who could minister to this person has had his or her fingers burned in the past. This is grievous for both parties. Clearly we need discernment in order to determine if the people we are reaching out to really seek wholeness.

Let's assume that the calling is clear and that ministry to a widow or fatherless child is the direction we are to pursue. Where do we start?

Ministering to Those in Distress

Let's look again at the main New Testament exhortation concerning orphans and widows, which is found in James 1:27: "Pure and undefiled religion before God and the Father is this: to visit orphans and widows in their trouble [*distress*, NIV]."

111

The word *visit* here implies to relieve and look out for. We are to help by looking out for not only physical needs, but spiritual, emotional and mental needs as well. In other words we need to minister to the whole person. And we are to do this because of their distress. Max Zerwick, in his *Grammatical Analysis of the Greek New Testament,* notes that the word *distress* means "whether in grief or want." This will require much patience and can best be achieved in an environment in which it is safe to be open and transparent.

We usually associate grief with traumatic happenings, but this is certainly not always the case. Parents, for instance, experience periods of grief as a child leaves one stage of development and launches into a new one. How many dads find it easy to watch their little sweetheart daughters slip into the teenage years almost overnight? Unless a father lets the grief out, he will forever be trying to keep her as his little girl, which can hinder her from becoming a mature adult.

Life is full of many such instances. Every time we experience loss in our lives, we endure successive periods of grief. This is normal and natural. Healing of grief is about letting go, allowing us to readjust to new circumstances. Unless you grieve, you make yourself a victim of the past. I know of instances of loss in my own life over which I did not grieve at the time. I found myself having to let the grief out years later.

For a widow to lose her husband or a child to lose his or her father is a mammoth change. This grief can be overwhelming and should not be treated lightly. If a child breaks his favorite toy, he comes crying to his mother and father and lets the grief out. It is all over in a short time. But to lose his father is life-threatening, cataclysmic, catastrophic. This level of grief will take much time to express fully. Likewise, when people marry they build their lives around the people they love. To be torn apart is shattering. The reality is so huge it can be embraced only little by little over the months and years. If grief is bottled inside, it will turn into anger and depression. If, on the other hand, we merely express emotions without processing them, we can end up on a dangerous path into self-pity.

Some insist that we have to come to a point when we stop grieving. In this regard, for instance, God gave the Israelites one month to grieve the death of Moses, then they had to move on. It is important to note, however, that they allowed—even encouraged—a full expression of grief during that time. Nothing was bottled up or left unexpressed. They surely felt pangs of loss later over his death, but they had given full vent to their sorrow. Note also how God expresses His own emotions in the Bible in full and very graphic ways.

Our society is quite different. It does not usually endorse expression of emotions. This leads to a "catch-22" situation: Emotions are pent up for fear they might burst forth inappropriately, but emotions would not burst forth inappropriately if they had not been pent up. The release of pent-up emotions is much like a dam that bursts when it is too full. It is very likely to happen if we do not process our feelings and root out any bitterness that may be adding to the pressure.

Consider this example. A woman feels a torrent of grief because her husband is gone. This is natural. But the grief is compounded by the fact that she has not dealt with the abandonment she felt from her father, who never really knew how to be there for her in the first place. The husband's death digs into that already existing wound even deeper. No matter how much she grieves, she cannot fully be healed until the deeper root is uncovered and she has forgiven her father for not being there when she needed him.

Anyone who has not experienced it may not understand the ongoing nature of grief. Every time a widow has to do one of her husband's duties, grief comes flooding back. Every time she wakes up in the morning, the reality hits her. She has no husband. If young children are in the home, they face equal devastation. Every time they see a man caring for his wife or children, the grief of what they do not have stabs them in the heart. Other reminders come every day—birthdays, anniversaries, Mother's Day, Father's Day, Christmas.

Children need a safe environment to express their grief both in the home and in the church. Unexpressed grief in children often leads to anger and rebellion. A simple touch or act of kindness reassures hurting people that they are loved in a world in which their sense of identity and belonging has been upended.

A child also needs to see that his mother has someone to support her in her grief, someone she can turn to when she is overwhelmed. If this does not happen, the child will likely either close off his own emotions in order to fill the void and comfort the grieving parent, or develop mechanisms of escape from the overwhelming circumstances. In both instances the child learns to fear emotion. He will not express grief for fear that the mountains of repressed emotion will come up and overwhelm him.

Children who have repressed grief will need help to overcome their fear of emotions so that eventually they can allow and value them.

God commands us not to afflict widows and the fatherless. Much hurt they receive is caused by a lack of understanding. For most of us, witnessing even small degrees of emotion is too much, for it exposes our own unaddressed hurts and wounds. If we are afraid of our own emotions, we will not be equipped to help someone else with his.

Many of us grew up in homes in which as children we absorbed too much emotional energy and consequently easily feel overwhelmed. Those who are willing to help are those who are prepared to go through the often excruciatingly painful process of having their own hearts exposed. Sanctification (the process of getting our hearts sorted out) is not a popular doctrine in a fast-paced world that puts so much value on external achievement, but it is the only way to achieve our own callings and to help others in theirs.

God's Plan

God's vision for every one of us is to become part of His Bride, without spot or wrinkle. With great determination and patience He sets about to bring us to this point. While we were yet sinners He loved us! In all of our uncleanness and filthiness He loved us!

Now, since we have become a part of the household of faith, His intense love for us causes Him to search out every spot and wrinkle. He lives inside of us and we have the confidence of knowing His blood and His Word continually cleanse us. The Word divides between soul and spirit, penetrating our inmost being (see Hebrews 4:12). The blood then cleanses everything brought into the light (see 1 John 1:7). God continues this process of healing throughout our entire lifetimes. Even if we are unfaithful, He remains faithful.

Just as He patiently and lovingly perseveres for us, He calls us to do the same with others. Indeed, this is the true essence of the Gospel. We need all the mercy we can get; therefore, we need to sow mercy at every opportunity. "Blessed are the merciful, for they shall obtain mercy" (Matthew 5:7). In the same way as He is faithful with us, He calls us to be faithful with the least among us. "Assuredly, I say to you, inasmuch as you did it to one of the least of these My brethren, you did it to Me" (Matthew 25:40).

Those who received good foundations of trust in childhood will be affected less severely and recover much more quickly. For many the only way to begin to restore trust is by sharing mutual pain:

> Blessed be the God and Father of our Lord Jesus Christ, the Father of mercies and God of all comfort, who comforts us in all our tribulation, that we may be able to comfort those who are in any trouble, with the comfort with which we ourselves are comforted by God.
>
> 2 Corinthians 1:3–4

This is why one of the best things we can do as individuals and churches to help widows and the fatherless is to become whole ourselves. It is from wholeness and healing in our own hearts that we are able to minister life to others. We would do well to strip away the many layers of denial that we build around our lives to convince us we are all right. James says we are to confess our sins to one another (see James 5:16). In modern vernacular we could say, "Confess your dysfunction to one another." This is something we usually go out of our way to avoid.

By creating an atmosphere of transparency and openness and love, a church is better able to minister to widows and the fatherless. In such an environment, no areas of grief, hurt or resentment can remain unexposed in a person's heart. They are forced to come to the light.

It is important for leaders to lead by example, taking the initiative to be transparent and open. When people can see you are real and human, just like them, you earn their respect. They feel they can trust you with their own hearts.

116

Availability and Reassurance

Ministering to a widow and her family requires commitment and sacrifice. Most likely they need someone to run to who is readily available. Being available is not necessarily a question of time; it can also mean the way a person's heart is open to listening and understanding. God always gives fair court trials. He wants widows and fatherless children to be able to share their hearts and be heard. You can give someone a lot of time, but still be unavailable emotionally. Once you have won trust by being patient and having a good listening ear, the time will come when you can begin to help them out of the pit. Remember, God is not in a hurry. He will spend whatever time is needed.

We must remember when ministering to anyone that we are being entrusted with one of God's children. This is an incredible privilege and must not be abused. When anyone trusts us with his or her inmost being, we must be careful to relate with gentleness and love. For victims of abandonment, rebuilding trust will often take years. Patience is a fruit of the Spirit; impatience is a work of the flesh.

Another area in which you should be extra careful with a widow and fatherless children is that of carrying out your word. They need you to be utterly dependable. If you say you will do something for them and then fail to do it, that is likely to hurt them and lead to feelings of betrayal. Give them abundant reassurance that you will not abandon them. Make sure you mean what you say.

Abandonment by death or divorce is such a traumatic change that those who experience it often fear any change at all. Changes that may seem small to others can seem very large to them. For this reason it is imperative to explain any changes that may affect them, particularly if it involves how much you can be there for them.

It is particularly important for orphans and widows to have the support and love of godly men who can help restore trust. They need to be men who are under the covering and direction of the church, who are secure in their marriages, who have good communication with their wives and who have their wives' support to help in this way.

In a world in which misguided sexuality is rampant, this may be a frightening concept. The reality is, however, that if widows and orphans are not fully embraced by the church and nurtured lovingly by its members, they will most likely end up in the grip of things that defile. Remember that Jesus let a prostitute express her love for Him by anointing His feet with expensive perfume and washing them with her tears.

The Reality of the Call

Someone who is not prepared to minister to distressed people will likely be swamped by their needs. People are often drawn to minister to widows and orphans because they have been through similar circumstances. They can provide comfort and empathy. This can be good but it can also be dangerous, particularly if the would-be helper has not become healed himself in those areas.

In order to bring life to another person, we need to be restored in the same areas ourselves. If this is not the case, it is still possible to be of some help to each other along the journey. It is important in such instances that both parties are determined to be fully healed and are not feeding each other's areas of wounding. It is best to seek help from those who are best able to give it.

Helping widows and the fatherless can be tough and demanding labor. Sometimes you may reach out to help only to be shocked when they lash out at you with unresolved anger. The expression of anger shows that love is touching areas of hardness. The path to healing is not an easy one. It is usually littered with debris that needs to be cleared away. In some places bridges need to be rebuilt. Often progress will be halted while major obstacles are overcome.

True, you will likely reap much of the hurt and anger they have bottled inside, but such ministry can also be greatly rewarding. Most often those who need help the most are those who appreciate it the most. To them you become a life-support system. If their trust has been betrayed in the past—whether actual or perceived betrayal—they will most likely thoroughly test you and will probably question your love, sincerity and genuineness over and over again. At the same time, they will probably feel bad for lashing out at the one who is there for them. Because families are often geared toward self-protection it can be hard to break through established family roles to restore trust. It is important to minister where God gives you the grace. Reach out to those to whom God specifically leads you.

We are to be led by the voice of God, not by human need. Our hearts must be set free from all need to be needed. As a Body we are called to minister to everyone in a general way, but there will be others to whom we may be called to minister more specifically. You must seek God's leading and discretion in this. In everything you need to be accountable to others, particularly to those in authority.

This also means that you must be able to set boundaries in your ministry to those in need. Parenting spiritual children is draining and hard work. For people who previously had no boundaries, even a few seem-

119

ingly nonrestrictive boundaries can turn their entire world upside-down. That is why you need confidence in knowing the leading of God in whatever you do. Too many boundaries can be interpreted as "You don't love me," or they remind the person of unjust demands from dysfunctional parents. That is why true Christian love must be the motivation behind everything you do.

God calls us to minister to all who are disadvantaged. He has prepared His table and calls us to bring in those who are poor and needy (see Luke 14:21). If widows and orphans need help to build confidence and trust, we need to be available. If they are weighed down with grief, we need to be available. Before we can do this, however, we must bring our own broken areas to the light and be willing to grow in openness and transparency ourselves.

This work is not for the fainthearted! May God guide us as we reach out to the wounded in His name.

thirteen

Feeling like a Nuisance

No one enjoys feeling like a nuisance. When you have been through trauma and have a host of unmet needs screaming for attention, worry about being thought a nuisance is a real concern. Many widows feel embarrassed about asking for help for themselves or their children. They think, *Who in his right mind wants to be bothered with so many problems?* Likewise, fatherless children have often learned to go it alone. Asking for help can take mountainous loads of courage. How easy it is to crush them with tentative or unwilling responses!

In a society in which the majority of people come from broken families, it is necessary for the Church to have answers. Let's look at a few of them.

Communicate Love

The first may be obvious. There is little reason to reach out if it is not done with love. It is important to realize, though, that love is communicated non-verbally as well as verbally. People pick up on it when non-verbal communications like attitudes or facial expressions say something different from what the spoken words say.

This may, in fact, be the main reason many widows and fatherless children feel as though they are nuisances—they pick up the non-verbal communications behind our good Christian exterior behaviors. Widows and the fatherless are very sensitive about this. They are well aware of being an inconvenience in their times of need.

When it is not possible for us to be available to help, we need to communicate that in ways that portray love and concern and do not create feelings of shame for having needs.

Help with Parenting

Widows often need help in the entirety of parenting. It is hard work at times to bring up children even in two-parent homes. It is much more difficult for a widow who has to be both mother and father, and she has half the strength to do it. Many women become completely defeated before they even begin. Parenting takes energy and strength. Just ask any mother who is left ragged at the end of the day.

A widow needs those who will stand with her in the struggles of parenting, giving her enough strength to be able to exercise God's rule in her home. She needs to be empowered to exercise godly and loving authority. (For further reading I recommend Ross Campbell's books, *How to Really Love Your Child* and *How to Really Love Your Teenager*. These books emphasize the importance of making sure a child's "love-tank" is full. The effectiveness of any type of discipline is apt to be minimal if a child does not feel loved.)

When children have been free to do as they please, controlling and manipulating their mother, they most certainly do not appreciate her rising from her position of helplessness and hopelessness to exercise godly authority. She needs to know that someone is standing with her as she fights against the continual urge to cave in under the pressures of her children.

Just being able to talk to someone else about an issue can impart the needed strength to address it and can also help to give her a clearer perspective. It is also a great help for her to know that she can seek out further counsel, fellowship or support should the situation become difficult. In such instances widows are often left thinking, *Did I do the right thing?* and *Was the reaction I received worth making the stand?*

The difficulty for her is that many times children hold deep anger toward her for supposedly allowing their father to die. In the case of divorce, they may blame her for the fact that their father left. Such anger can exist even in cases when it is clear that she was abandoned through no fault of her own.

Additionally, children sometimes idolize a parent who has left. This means that the absent parent—their memory of him—has great power to influence the values and perceptions of the children. It is helpful for a widow to speak out good things about their father for them to hear. It can remove their need to have to defend him. The same is true for divorcees, as hard as that may be. The alternative too often is angry and rebellious children who can make a mother feel as though she has lost not only her husband but her children as well.

Dishonor in the Home

One other word here about divorce. Husbands are supposed to model honor and respect for their wives before their children. When a husband leaves his family, he dishonors them, causing seeds of dishonor to be sown in the home.

Increasingly in today's churches our main concern with the fatherless is to try to control their rebellious behavior in church services. That is not a case of making them a ministry priority; that is a case of dealing with a nuisance. Yet we are talking about a rapidly increasing proportion of our society. We simply must come up with a biblical strategy to reach them with the care they need.

The best place to start is to let these children see people in the church, particularly men, showing honor and respect to their mother. This gives them a model of how to treat their mother and how to treat women in general. Churches need to esteem single mothers and encourage them to establish boundaries, especially when their children are treating them in a disrespectful way.

Help Widows Find Meaningful Function

When Paul addressed Timothy on the issue of caring for widows, he was very clear about their care:

Honor widows who are really widows. But if any widow has children or grandchildren, let them first learn to show piety at home and to repay their parents; for this is good and acceptable before God. Now she who is really a widow, and left alone, trusts in God and continues in supplications and prayers night and day. But she who lives in pleasure is dead while she lives. And these things command, that they may be blameless. But if anyone does not provide for his own, and especially for those of his household, he has denied the faith and is worse than an unbeliever.

Do not let a widow under sixty years old be taken into the number, and not unless she has been the wife of one man [*has been faithful to her husband*, NIV], well reported for good works: if she has brought up children, if she has lodged strangers, if she has washed the saints' feet, if she has relieved the afflicted, if she has diligently followed every good work.

But refuse the younger widows; for when they have begun to grow wanton against Christ, they desire to marry, having condemnation because they have cast off their first faith. And besides they learn to be idle, wandering about from house to house, and not only idle but also gossips and busybodies, saying things which they ought not. Therefore I desire that the younger widows marry, bear children, manage the house, give no opportunity to the adversary to speak reproachfully. For some have already turned aside after Satan. If any believing man or woman has widows, let them relieve them, and do not let the church be burdened, that it may relieve those who are really widows.

1 Timothy 5:3–16

These regulations may sound strict, but they actually serve to honor widows. By making it clear who is to be responsible for her and what role she is to play, Paul removed the nuisance factor. She is to be honored by being cared for by her family or her church, and she is honored by being given a clearly defined role to carry out. Good boundaries lead to security and a greater sense of being loved.

Part of restoration and provision for widows and the fatherless is to help them find ways to give meaningful input into the lives of their families and churches. To live life without some sort of function, job, purpose or career is demeaning to anyone.

It is God's plan for us as humans to have function, purpose and destiny. One of the reasons there are so many disgruntled people in churches today is because there is failure for them to have meaningful purpose or functions. Idle people grumble. For many widows in our day, their main task is bringing up their children. As they overcome the seemingly insurmountable hurdles involved in managing their own households, it is God's desire to entrust them with other varied responsibilities within the church. When the Bible says the saints are to be equipped to do the work of ministry, it means all the saints, not just some. This includes widows, divorcees and the fatherless.

I particularly encourage widows to get involved in something that develops them personally. It may be something they have not done before or something they have always wanted to do. Some examples could be art or dance classes, learning a musical instrument, Bible correspondence courses, physical sport or activity, hobbies of any description. This gives something positive on which to focus.

Many feel it is selfish to do something for themselves, particularly if there is a limited budget; surely the needs of children should come first. Children's needs are important, but sometimes the best thing a widow can do for her children is to model a life of purpose and destiny in the midst of emptiness and loneliness. Children will likely follow any example given in this regard and seek to enjoy life by searching out opportunities to develop their own interests. On the other hand, it is important that activity not be used as a means of denying or escaping from the reality of the situation; it should give a positive focus in the midst of it.

Am I a Nuisance?

Finally, let me give a word of reassurance to widows and the fatherless themselves. God does not see you as a nuisance. Those who consider you as such are not portraying the heart of God. But do not judge them for this. To God you are wonderfully and fearfully made. No matter how great your needs, He has made provision through the cross. He is intensely zealous to see you fully restored and whole.

Sometimes loving boundaries laid down by those who care for you may seem to make your world feel torn apart or turned upside down. Please understand that sometimes well-meaning people may not fully understand. At other times they may have the difficult task of having to minister truth to you. It may feel like a pneumatic drill, but it is necessary to break up wrong foundations in your life. At times you may feel like lashing out. It is no easy task for anyone to have to break up old foundations and lay new ones.

Never forget, precious one, you are worth it. No matter how much work living demands, you are worth it. Don't feel shamed because of your needs. At times your needs may seem to gobble up people, but they will never gobble up God. As you learn to focus, trust and abide in Him, more and more you will come to rest on the fact that His sufficiency is much, much greater than your insufficiency. And that is one of the greatest lessons of the Kingdom.

fourteen

Lonely Husbands, Lonely Wives and Lonely Children

As churches become equipped to minister effectively to their widows and fatherless children, they must also turn attention to the multitudes of husbands, wives and children who are lonely even though they are part of a secure family unit.

Loneliness is a pervasive problem in our society. We can see it everywhere but it is rarely acknowledged or spoken of. It has become unacceptable to speak of loneliness, since it exposes everyone else's cover-up.

The truth is most people are lonely, even those of the household of faith. Remember that Elijah, one of the most powerful, anointed prophets in history, fell into a chasm of loneliness. Christians often feel as though it would be a denial of faith if we admitted to being lonely. After all, we have Jesus, don't we? So we cover it up by trying to pretend it is not there. But ignoring loneliness will not make it go away.

Many people decide that marriage is the answer to loneliness. They crave a marriage partner to fill the deep void in their hearts. This will never work because only God can answer the cry of the human heart. A couple in marriage can be so far apart emotionally that though they sleep in the same bed, they are every bit as lonely and isolated as before they were married. In fact, more so, because now they are lonely in company, where they think they ought not feel that way.

It is the same thing that people do with ministry: They hold it in a too highly elevated position. They think that if they could just be released into the ministry God has given them, then life would be great. They may not realize that to enter the service to which God has called them might become one of the hardest things they have ever done.

Society promotes this concept of marriage as a solution in the sense that we esteem marriage as a status symbol, somewhat like a badge we wear. If you are married you are successful, you have arrived. But marriage is not a measure of status. To treat it as such is to treat it as an end, when, in fact, it is the beginning of something new. In addition, this view subconsciously looks down on those who are unmarried as inferior. Could we include the apostle Paul in this category? What about the widow Anna who served God in the Temple with night-and-day intercession?

The answer to loneliness does not lie in any particular lifestyle; the answer lies in fellowship with God. He is a jealous God and will not let anything or anyone else come before Him. God wants His Bride restored. He will no longer allow "church as usual" when most sit in cocoons of loneliness.

How, then, do we help those who find themselves in lonely family situations? We begin by adjusting our thinking.

We probably recognize, for instance, the isolation that divorced individuals have to face. Going through divorce is traumatic enough, but in most cases there were also years where one or both partners were unloved, unwanted, mistreated or ignored in subtle or not so subtle ways. We understand that restoring such a person is going to take a long time. The process of rebuilding trust will have to be worked out in everyday relationships until the years of being conditioned to neglect are overcome.

We probably do not recognize, though, that untold thousands live in marriages and families like this. How often, really, do we see the plight of lonely couples and lonely children who live in homes where the marriage covenant has not been severed? As tragic as divorce is, at least it brings the situation to some kind of resolution. The people we are talking about live in hellish isolation every day. They live lives of quiet, hidden desperation.

Typically these are Christian women married to unsaved husbands. It may sound as though I am singling out men as the ones causing this situation, but I am not. While it is perhaps more common for a wife to be in this situation, this problem exists extensively among Christian couples. I am writing this chapter to help both marriage partners. God feels their pain, their loneliness and their isolation.

We might, now, look with a different perspective. And suppose we realize that someone in our midst is lost in loneliness. What is our response to be?

Our Response

As the Church we must recognize and help these people. They form a huge portion of our congregations. Many need help acknowledging that they are indeed lonely because their denial mechanisms are very strong. Many times women or children do not ask for help because they are afraid of their husbands' or parents' possible reactions. Those who can admit their loneliness usually feel too ashamed to admit it publicly. They are apprehensive about what sort of reactions they may receive.

Will they be heard?
Will they be helped?
Will they be judged?

Jesus weeps over the lonely lives in our churches. He sees them and feels their pain. How often do we? The word *widow* actually means "desolate and empty." How many people may there be like this who are, in fact, married?

The Unloved Wife

For an example of a lonely wife in Scripture, let us turn to the life of Leah, the wife of Jacob. Jacob had two wives, Leah and Rachel, who were sisters. It was through the trickery of his uncle Laban that Jacob found himself married to both of Laban's daughters. The Bible says that "Leah's eyes were delicate, but Rachel was beautiful of form and appearance" (Genesis 29:17).

Jacob loved Rachel more than Leah. Many assume Rachel was more attractive than Leah, but this may not be the case. Some translations use the word *weak* to describe Leah's eyes. But the word can also be translated *delicate* as it is above. If this translation is correct, it could be describing Leah's attractiveness.

Imagine being married to two jealous sisters who are constantly competing to earn your favor! I think Jacob must have been an amazing individual to live with ongoing sibling rivalry, especially when the siblings were both adults. God surely knew how to refine Jacob's character!

Because Leah was unloved, God opened her womb. She bore Jacob his first four children, including Levi, the ancestor of the priests, and Judah, the ancestor of King David and of the Messiah, Jesus. God sees and hears the cry of those who are unloved. Through bearing Jacob's children, Leah hoped to win his approval.

> When the LORD saw that Leah was unloved, He opened her womb; but Rachel was barren. So Leah conceived and bore a son, and she called his name Reuben; for she said, "The LORD has surely looked on my affliction. Now therefore, my husband will love me." Then she conceived again and bore a son, and said, "Because the LORD has heard that I am unloved, He has therefore given me this son also." And she called his name Simeon. She conceived again and bore a son, and said, "Now this time my husband will become attached to me, because I have borne him three sons." Therefore his name was called Levi. And she conceived again and bore a son, and said, "Now I will praise the LORD." Therefore she called his name Judah.
>
> Genesis 29:31–35

After bearing Jacob four children Leah thought she would finally win the approval of her husband, so she praised the Lord.

Because Rachel could not bear children, she gave Jacob her maid Bilhah, who bore him two sons, Dan and Naphtali:

And Bilhah conceived and bore Jacob a son. Then Rachel said, "God has judged my case; and He has also heard my voice and given me a son." Therefore she called his name Dan. And Rachel's maid Bilhah conceived again and bore Jacob a second son. Then Rachel said, "With great wrestlings I have wrestled with my sister, and indeed I have prevailed." So she called his name Naphtali.

Genesis 30:5–8

Leah followed suit and gave Jacob her maid Zilpah, who bore two sons, Gad and Asher. Leah then had two more sons, Issachar and Zebulun.

And Leah said, "God has endowed me with a good endowment; now my husband will dwell with me, because I have borne him six sons."

Genesis 30:20

Finally God opened Rachel's womb.

Then God remembered Rachel, and God listened to her and opened her womb. And she conceived and bore a son, and said, "God has taken away my reproach." So she called his name Joseph, and said, "The LORD shall add to me another son."

Genesis 30:22–24

The desire in a woman's heart is that one day she will be loved and cherished as number one in the heart of the man she marries. God intends for wives to hold this place in their husbands' hearts, but it does not always happen. Leah was not number one to Jacob; Rachel was always his first love. Many wives are like Leah. They spend their entire lives striving with the things that hold first place—sports, alcohol, careers, other women, ministry, television, etc.

133

Just as God ministered to Leah and made her fruitful, so He wants to minister to lonely wives and restore their marriages to what He intended them to be. First Corinthians 7:13–14 states clearly that even if a husband is unsaved, the reality of Christ in the wife sanctifies him. The word *sanctify* in these verses connotes causing change that has permanence. Such is the power of the indwelling Christ.

If you are a lonely wife, reach out for the Lord to increase your faith in His indwelling presence. He alone can change your husband. Be the best partner you can be, but put your faith in God's ability to change and transform him rather than your ability to perform perfectly. He will not overthrow the free will of your husband; however, your prayers can remove the blockages to his hearing God's prompting.

And then consider this: What changes do you think God might want to do in your own heart to help you draw closer to Him? Do you feel that you have to compete for His love as well? Many lonely people feel that they have to go to great lengths to try and obtain their earthly fathers' love and approval. Every child yearns to be the apple of his or her daddy's eye, to be treated with tenderness and treasured as valuable. If you are one of those who never knew this love, God wants to reveal His unconditional love to you as your heavenly Father. I encourage you to ask Him to reveal it. It is a request He loves to answer. And what is more, you do not have to do anything to earn it.

Loved and Fruitful

God *saw* that Leah was not loved. This is our example to follow. We must see the many in our ranks who are likewise unloved. May God give us eyes to see. Second,

He opened Leah's womb. In other words He made her fruitful. God calls us to open our hearts to minister to those who are unloved. By doing so we make them fruitful to minister to others (particularly their families) and to God.

The Church is called to be the Bride of Christ. As His Bride we will no longer be clothed with shame but will radiate His glory. But first we must do as He does and respond to those who are destitute in our midst. His work of restoration in the lives of lonely wives and lonely children (as well as others) will testify of His ultimate work of bringing the entire Church into glory. "For the LORD shall build up Zion; He shall appear in His glory. He shall regard the prayer of the destitute, and shall not despise their prayer" (Psalm 102:16–17).

It is time to let the Lord rebuild and restore the brokenhearted through us. "Those from among you shall build the old waste places; you shall raise up the foundations of many generations; and you shall be called the Repairer of the Breach, the Restorer of Streets to Dwell In" (Isaiah 58:12).

fifteen

God's Original Design

Here is one woman's experience of divorce:

> After my husband left, my social standing plummeted—
> on several fronts. Forget the luxury of an escalator to es-
> cort me down smoothly to my new position. Instead the
> supports were whipped out from under me and I came
> crashing down. I had to explore my new surroundings
> in a rather dazed and disorientated state. Simple things
> that I used to take for granted were now a struggle, as
> feelings of inferiority and intimidation took over. It felt
> a bit like being a kid in a world full of towering adults.
>
> The problem was compounded by the fact that the
> humiliation happened on a number of different fronts
> one after the other. First of all there was the disapproval
> I felt from my parents for causing the family name to
> be shamed. Then there was the disappointment from all
> my friends who used to relate to my husband and me
> as one entity. My religious friends were awkward, their
> theological perceptions causing them to despise both
> divorce and divorcees. My children were angry with me
> for letting Dad leave. And as if that was not enough,

there was the humiliation of having to change all my official documents (bankbook, insurance policies), to divide important assets and to become dependent on welfare.

All in all it was a very public humiliation.

In order to bring restoration to marriages it is first necessary to ask the question, Why are so many marriages ending in divorce? At present divorce has reached epidemic proportions both inside and outside the Church. Divorce had no place in God's original plan for marriage. How then do we deal with the many divorces between Christians today?

Divorce, a Corporate Problem

In 1 Corinthians 7:15 Paul says that if an unbeliever leaves a marriage, his or her spouse is not under bondage to the one who left and is free to remarry: "If the unbeliever departs, let him depart; a brother or sister is not under bondage in such cases. But God has called us to peace."

The instructions for marriages between believers are quite different:

> Now to the married I command, yet not I but the Lord: A wife is not to depart from her husband. But even if she does depart, let her remain unmarried or be reconciled to her husband. And a husband is not to divorce his wife.
>
> 1 Corinthians 7:10–11

The Church is called to hold divorcees accountable and to assist and encourage couples in the process of reconciliation. Reconciliation is only possible if both parties are prepared to work it out. The tense of the verb *reconciled* in the Greek is aorist imperative. This indicates a command, not a suggestion.

Despite this biblical mandate, divorce among Christians continues to ravage the lives of many. Perhaps it is due to the prevailing spirit of unbelief that infects much of the Body of Christ. Statistics show that there is next to no difference between the world and the Church in areas of sexual immorality and divorce.

The extent of divorce in the Church is so widespread that I do not believe it can be considered a private issue, involving just the affected family and friends. It affects the whole Body. Thus, it becomes a challenge for us all to examine our own hearts in the light of Scripture. You will recall that sanctification is a process through which our hearts are transformed by death and rebirth through the cross. Divorce is a direct result of this process breaking down. Unhealed wounds in the person's heart cause breakdowns in relationships until they are deemed irreconcilable. This pattern will continue in relationship after relationship if it is not properly addressed.

If we worked corporately to help these parts of the Body that are so relationally vulnerable; if we helped people early on before situations were deemed irreconcilable; if we were willing to follow the many relational exhortations to the Church, such as Paul's directives above regarding reconciliation, there would be few, if any, divorces.

Still, the power of the cross is able to reconcile lives, no matter how big the breach. Unhealed wounds can be brought to the light and healed.

Jesus wants to reach in and heal the wounds at a root level rather than just deal with surface problems. Permanent change is possible only if you deal with the root cause. Unless this is accomplished, patterns of marriage, divorce and remarriage are likely to recur. The pattern of divorce also passes down from one generation to the next. Children from divorced homes are more likely to experience divorce themselves.

One major cause of divorce relates to a person's relationship with the opposite sex parent. Deep hurts and unforgiveness, resentment and bitterness, expectations and perceptions toward the opposite sex parent are projected onto the person's spouse. It is areas of the heart such as these that need to be exposed to the light, enabling the process of sanctification to happen. It takes enormous amounts of strength to deal with deep heart issues. Such ones need the loving nurture and help of those around them.

We simply have to face it. The present plague of divorce will be stopped only by a corporate response. This response will require us all to examine the root issues in our own hearts. It will require us to understand and embrace the fullness of God's intentions for covenant relationships.

God's Pattern for Marriage

When the Pharisees questioned Jesus about divorce, He responded by pointing them back to the beginning. God's original purpose and design for marriage was recorded in the book of Genesis immediately after Eve was created. The book of Genesis is, in fact, the book of beginnings. "Therefore shall a man leave his father and his mother, and shall cleave unto his wife: and they shall be one flesh" (Genesis 2:24, KJV). Every passage of Scripture that gives additional revelation or insight about marriage is to be viewed with God's original intent in mind. The sequence recorded here is clear: *leave*, *cleave* and then *become one flesh*.

Leaving and Cleaving

Sadly, many are not able to cleave to their marriage partners because in their hearts they have not left home. In fact, the reason divorce is so rampant in our Western societies is because many couples are unable to truly cleave. And the reason they are unable to cleave is because they have so many unaddressed heart issues from the past.

It is our relationships with our parents, particularly fathers, that call us forth to life, giving us identity. Without knowing unconditional love from our parents, we become handicapped in who we are called to be. This means that there is an inability to meet with a marriage partner as a whole, healthy being. Instead the unmet need for parental affection and nurture is sought from the marriage. This prevents true cleaving.

The need for identity and acceptance from our parents is so strong that without it we spend the rest of our lives seeking it in whatever form we think may meet our needs. If this is the case, we have never truly left home. Many fail to see this about themselves because they grew up in "good" homes where they were loved. The truth is that any areas in which parents are not whole in their own hearts are areas in which they are not able to give themselves in a healthy and truly loving manner; hence, children are abandoned in precisely those areas. When children have "good" parents it is very hard for them to see this.

In the Garden of Eden God singled out two trees, the Tree of Life and the Tree of the Knowledge of Good and Evil. This latter tree, from which Adam and Eve ate, bore bad fruit for them; eating it resulted in the fall of mankind. It is the good side of this tree that is the most deceptive, simply because it seems good to us. Much religious activity is rooted in the good side of this tree. Also much of our perception of what is good has its origins here, including our perception of good parents.

I say this not to make us critical of our parents but rather to help us see the areas of abandonment in our hearts that have never been addressed and prevent us from truly leaving home. Transformation must come in these areas to enable us to cleave to our marriage partners. Healing comes as we allow God into those painful areas of our hearts that have been closed, locked and barred. The only way is to face the pain and not hide from it.

God brings restoration both through the power of the Holy Spirit and through our being vulnerable to others, letting Him minister to our hearts through other people. Many want to avoid being vulnerable to others, preferring to let God alone do the work. Most likely these people have areas of hurt and unforgiveness in their hearts that prevent them from being vulnerable and open. We need to ask God to:

1. Remove the blockages through forgiveness.
2. Do the work of transformation and healing in our hearts by death and rebirth through the cross.
3. Give us strength to hold our hearts open to Him and others, including being vulnerable to those with whom we find it most difficult.

Again, all of this is possible only through the power of the cross. The above process enables us to leave home fully and cleave as God intended. By going through this process, married couples enrich their marriages way beyond what they have known.

The Glory of a One-Flesh Relationship

When God says the two shall become one flesh, He is referring to much more than physical intimacy. *One flesh* means being able to meet whole person to whole person. This is not just a physical union but a union of our whole beings—spirit, soul and body. The glory of this is something beyond what most have ever tasted or experienced.

When the Pharisees questioned Jesus about divorce, He told them of God's original design found in the book of Genesis. They replied, "Why then did Moses command to give a certificate of divorce, and to put her away?" (Matthew 19:7). Jesus answered them, "Moses, because of the hardness of your hearts, permitted you to divorce your wives, but from the beginning it was not so" (verse 8).[1]

Moses permitted divorce because of the people's hardness of heart. The word in the Greek for *hardness of heart* means specifically "destitution of spiritual perception." The reason people divorce is because they have never had a true vision of what God created marriage to be. Those who can see (who have spiritual perception of) the glory of what God created a one-flesh relationship to be, do not consider the process of leaving and cleaving too painful or inconvenient to work through. If the plague of divorces is to be stopped, true vision of what

1. Another source of judgment for divorcees is the unbiblical teaching that forbids them to remarry until their former marriage partners die. This teaching is based primarily on the words of Jesus and has been the topic of much theological controversy over the centuries.

In Jesus' day there were different schools of thought about what actions gave a man the right to write a certificate of divorce. Some believed that even minor things, such as bad cooking, meant a man was able to divorce his wife. Jesus stated that if a person divorces for any less a reason than adultery, he or she is committing adultery. Jesus' intention, however, was not to put victims of divorce under bondage. Rather, He was addressing those who were deceitfully manipulating themselves out of marriage.

The reasons for many of the misinterpretations concerning Jesus' words about divorce come about, firstly, because the words are not considered in their biblical context and, secondly, because they are not considered in their cultural context.

God intended marriage to be must be restored to the Body of Christ. We are called to demonstrate this to the world.

In saying this I must also make it clear that the way to walk in the full glory of marriage is not to strive after an impossible ideal. God's original design for marriage is unobtainable in our own strength. All of our striving must come to death, as well as all of our false expectations and ideals, as we learn to rest in Him and let Him bring all good things to pass.

Building a good marriage requires patience, love, tolerance and acceptance with your partner and yourself. The enemy loves to stir up condemnation about our failure—or our spouses' failure!—to be good marriage partners, making us feel as though we can never measure up to what God requires. Self-condemnation leads to continual striving, and ultimately to discouragement and defeat. When we learn to rest in Him and cease striving in the flesh, He brings us into glories we never dreamed of.

Adam and Loneliness

After God created Adam, He allowed him to share in the diversity of His creation by letting him name every animal that walked the earth. Despite the fact that God had created a world with so much color, beauty and diversity, Adam was lonely. There was still a part of him that remained unfulfilled. This is an amazing thing considering that God, by sharing His creation with Adam, was sharing Himself. By this Adam would have come to know wonderful, rich fellowship with Almighty God. I believe God allowed Adam to experience loneliness because it was loneliness that led him into fellowship with Eve. When we see that Adam was unfulfilled despite the fullness of His fellowship with God, we can begin to understand the full glory that God intended for marriage.

Adam's fellowship with God led him to Eve. From his fellowship with Eve came greater fulfillment in relating to God. This in turn led to greater fulfillment as man and wife. This is how God designed it. Relationship with God must be the priority. It was when Adam esteemed his wife above the Word of God that the Fall happened. One of the best things men or women can do to improve their marriages is to become passionate seekers of God.

A Revolutionary Revelation

Why am I including this study of marriage in a book on widows and orphans? First, because healthy married couples can become a powerful force to minister directly to widows and the fatherless, and, second, because widows and orphans suffer even further when other parts of the Body suffer.

I cannot say this more clearly: The reason there is so much divorce in the Church is because, as a corporate entity, we have lost the revelation of the glory of marriage. If even secure marriages would begin to walk in the fullness of what God has available, I believe it would have an impact on the whole Body of Christ and the world itself. It would cause the divorce rate to come tumbling down. It would encourage single women who have been abused and abandoned by men to open their hearts and seek what is truly from God. Trust would be restored. It would also model something to a generation that rejects marriage. People would embrace marriage as the beautiful and fulfilling state God created it to be.

If you are a widow or fatherless child, God wants to revolutionize your concept of marriage and fatherhood—which can be wonderful beyond anything you could ever imagine. In the midst of brokenness and pain this may seem impossible, but nothing is impossible with God.

The truth is, if you have suffered loss in a particular area, then you are the very one to carry with great determination and purpose the revelation of what could be. If, for instance, your father left when you were young and you were able to build a father/daughter relationship with a godly man in the church, then you may treasure the concept of fatherhood even more than those who had fathers at home. Likewise, widows often come to value marriage with greater understanding—not only because they are lonely, but because they recognize the significance and depth of what they are without.

Some of those who have been the most devastated by broken marriages will arise with this God-given revelation, become fully restored and further revolutionize the Church's concept and understanding of marriage. They will champion a cause, a foundational message, one that issues from the very heart of God.

The impact of this will be far-reaching. When God's order is restored to the marriage relationship, causing it to come into line with His original design, one of the enemy's major strongholds will be destroyed from our midst. This will result in such an increase in our level of authority that the gates of hell will tremble, knowing their destruction is imminent.

Part 4

Stories of Faith, Hope for the Future

sixteen

Uncommon Faith

Some of the most significant happenings recorded in biblical history have been the result of widows displaying uncommon faith, courage and sacrifice. It seems that God likes to cause those whom others consider as the least to play the most significant parts in the outworking of His purposes in the earth. In this chapter we will consider some of these examples.

Ruth: A Type of the True Church

This young woman was not even an Israelite and yet she became the great-grandmother of King David, forming part of the lineage of Jesus. Her story is recorded in the book of Ruth.

> Now it came to pass, in the days when the judges ruled, that there was a famine in the land. And a certain man of Bethlehem, Judah, went to dwell in the country of Moab, he and his wife and his two sons. The name of the man

was Elimelech, the name of his wife was Naomi, and the names of his two sons were Mahlon and Chilion— Ephrathites of Bethlehem, Judah. And they went to the country of Moab and remained there. Then Elimelech, Naomi's husband, died; and she was left, and her two sons. Now they took wives of the women of Moab: the name of the one was Orpah, and the name of the other Ruth. And they dwelt there about ten years. Then both Mahlon and Chilion also died; so the woman survived her two sons and her husband.

Ruth 1:1–5

When Naomi heard that the famine in Israel was over she decided to return. She set off with her two daughters-in-law. As she went she tried to persuade Ruth and Orpah to return to Moab so they could find other husbands. As a destitute and aged widow she could offer them no future in Israel. Orpah decided to return to Moab. Ruth's response was:

> "Entreat me not to leave you, or to turn back from following after you; for wherever you go, I will go; and wherever you lodge, I will lodge; your people shall be my people, and your God, my God. Where you die, I will die, and there will I be buried. The Lord do so to me, and more also, if anything but death parts you and me."

Ruth 1:16–17

When Ruth made her decision to go with her mother-in-law, she gave up everything she had known. How easy it is in the midst of crisis to return to that which is safe, known and familiar! Ruth had the courage to give up everything she knew for an unknown future, an unknown land, people and customs, and an unknown God.

The custom of the day was for a brother to marry his brother's widow. Since Naomi had no more sons, this

150

was not possible. She was too old to marry and have sons, and even if she did, Ruth would have had to wait years before one would be old enough to marry. When Ruth left Moab and went with Naomi, she was giving up her desire for remarriage and trusting herself implicitly to Naomi's God.

In Israel Ruth served Naomi by working in the fields. Because of this God was able to work a miracle. Ruth became the wife of a wealthy relative of Naomi named Boaz. They became the great-grandparents of King David—a man after God's own heart, a man who prepared a throne upon which Jesus Himself would sit. His ministry reached beyond time into eternity. Is it only coincidence that in his heritage was a godly woman named Ruth?

Throughout Israel's history as the chosen people of God, they strayed continually after other gods and consequently drank the waters of bitterness over and over again. God was about to show Israel favor through a non-Israelite daughter-in-law who became a type of the Church. The true Church will serve Israel even when everything is turned against her. The false church will turn away like Orpah, thinking only of her own interests. To serve Israel in these times will require huge sacrifices, devotion, faith and courage. Particularly when world opinion is going to be blatantly and violently against her.

I believe widows and the fatherless are to play a key role in imparting this level of faith to the Body of Christ. Widows who have stood in the midst of crises and who hold unwavering faith in God have an understanding of devotion and sacrifice many of us lack. God sees this and knows they are going to be some of His most trustworthy servants in His end-time army.

Dear widow, if you are reading this book, let me encourage you not to give up even if you are in the midst of great crisis and need. The highest places of honor in God's Kingdom are reserved for such as you. You may have no strength to persevere, but if you trust Him, He will help you to overcome. Don't let self-pity overcome you by causing you to compare your life and your lot with others. You can do something they cannot: stand victorious against the odds. Uncommon faith is shown by uncommon sacrifice in the midst of crisis and adversity. Ruth demonstrated this. With God's help you can, too.

The Widow of Zarephath: Believing for Miracles

The next example of uncommon faith displayed by a widow is found in 1 Kings 17. Like Ruth, this widow was not even an Israelite, but a foreigner who lived in Sidon, a city north of Israel. This poor widow fed and housed Elijah, one of Israel's greatest prophets, during a time of great famine.

> Then the word of the LORD came to him, saying, "Arise, go to Zarephath, which belongs to Sidon, and dwell there. See, I have commanded a widow there to provide for you." So he arose and went to Zarephath. And when he came to the gate of the city, indeed a widow was there gathering sticks. And he called to her and said, "Please bring me a little water in a cup, that I may drink." And as she was going to get it, he called to her and said, "Please bring me a morsel of bread in your hand."
>
> Then she said, "As the LORD your God lives, I do not have any bread, only a handful of flour in a bin, and a little oil in a jar; and see, I am gathering a couple of sticks that I may go in and prepare it for myself and my son, that we may eat it, and die."
>
> And Elijah said to her, "Do not fear; go and do as you have said, but make me a small cake from it first, and

bring it to me; and afterward make some for yourself and your son. For thus says the LORD God of Israel: 'The bin of flour shall not be used up, nor shall the jar of oil run dry, until the day the LORD sends rain on the earth.'"

So she went away and did according to the word of Elijah; and she and he and her household ate for many days. The bin of flour was not used up, nor did the jar of oil run dry, according to the word of the LORD which He spoke by Elijah.

1 Kings 17:8–16

What this woman possessed was tiny—a handful of flour and a little oil. Despite the fact she had little, God used it to sustain one of the most powerful ministries of all time. Elijah was the prophet who stood against the entire nation of Israel at a time when they had fallen into great apostasy. Because of the enormity of his task, Elijah was equipped with great supernatural power. He was able to call down fire from heaven and cause the heavens to be shut up, giving no rain for three and a half years.

God's end-time ministries likewise are called to confront great darkness. God will entrust them accordingly with great power. The days coming upon the earth will be tumultuous. Everything that can be shaken will be shaken (see Hebrews 12:26). In the midst of such upheaval God intends to use people like the widow of Zarephath who are prepared to employ uncommon faith. These people will be the unlikely heroes whose testimony will be recorded in heaven's history books.

This woman sacrificed her own fears about providing for herself and her son to obey God's command through Elijah. Her little amounted to much when yielded to God! She was prepared to take the risk of faith and obey God. Do not believe the enemy's lies. A little, mixed with faith, can have earth-shaking results.

Why is it that God frequently uses the destitute to accomplish His purposes? Because being destitute means that you have nothing to lose and must be dependent on God alone. What would this woman have lost if the flour and oil had not been replaced? She was about to die anyway.

In our day there are people to whom God has given much. They have the ability to help people relationally and yet are reluctant to endure the pain of helping others. Those who are destitute do not have much to live for and do not have as much to lose. Whereas others are reluctant, they may be prepared to help people at their own expense and cost. That is why widows and the fatherless are so important in this harvest hour. They will be some of the best harvesters, giving themselves time and again to help salvage wrecked and helpless lives in order to bring them safely into the arms of a loving Savior.

Jesus commented on the widow of Zarephath in Luke 4:24–26:

> Then He said, "Assuredly, I say to you, no prophet is accepted in his own country. But I tell you truly, many widows were in Israel in the days of Elijah, when the heaven was shut up three years and six months, and there was a great famine throughout all the land; but to none of them was Elijah sent except to Zarephath, in the region of Sidon, to a woman who was a widow."

God sent Elijah to her because she was willing to obey the word of the Lord. Faith is what made her stand apart from every other widow in Israel. Faith is not something you work up by trying to believe. Rather it is simple trust. God would not rely on any widow in Israel because Israel had fallen into idolatry and was serving foreign gods.

Widows have plenty of opportunity to learn to trust Him. Sometimes that may be the most difficult thing they will ever do. Many have already found God to be trustworthy in so many ways. The widow of Zarephath did—every day. Every day God performed a miracle. Simple trust says, "God, this mess I am in is too big for me to handle, but I choose to trust You to help me get through it one day at a time." To trust God continually, day after day, takes more faith than believing Him for a truckload of flour and a tank of oil. Remember when God had a need to feed and house Elijah the prophet, it was a widow He sent him to.

After God had supernaturally provided for the widow of Zarephath, a great tragedy happened: Her son died. Having already lost her husband, she was unable to restrain her anger and laid the blame on Elijah. "What have I to do with you, O man of God? Have you come to me to bring my sin to remembrance, and to kill my son?" (1 Kings 17:18). Elijah took her dead son to his own upper room and prayed, stretching his body over the corpse three times. The son came to life. Elijah's uncommon faith caused the tragedy of this woman's circumstance to be turned around. He did this even though she laid the blame for her predicament on him. This is the first record in Scripture of someone being raised from the dead.

After Elijah was taken up to heaven, Elisha received his mantle and continued to minister in like manner. There are two instances in Elisha's ministry that are particularly relevant to widows. In the first a woman's husband died (see 2 Kings 4:1–7). The husband had unpaid debts. As recompense for the debt her two sons were to be taken as slaves. She told Elisha her predicament. After finding out that she had a jar of oil he told her to collect as many jars as she could and start pouring oil into them. The oil kept flowing until every jar was full.

Then he told her to sell the oil to pay off the debt and to live off the rest.

Once again God took a little and multiplied it greatly. Most significantly, however, this woman was able to keep from losing her two sons to slavery. By this she, too, was set free from the prospects of a pitiful existence without sons to provide for her.

The second instance in Elisha's life relevant to widows is one that involves a married woman (see 2 Kings 4:8–17). This woman had no sons and her husband was old. This meant that once he died, she would be a widow with no one to support her. This woman provided Elisha with a room where he could stay when he would pass through her region. Because of this, Elisha asked if anything could be done in return for the favor she had shown him. When he found out that she had no son and that her husband was old, he gave her a promise from God that within a year she would give birth to a son. In response she said to him, "No, my lord. Man of God, do not lie to your maid-servant!" (2 Kings 4:16).

After one year she gave birth to a son as prophesied. The child grew but then became sick and died. The woman put the dead boy on Elisha's bed and went immediately to find him. In her great distress this woman sought out Elisha, the one who had given her the promise. Perhaps she had heard of Elijah raising a widow's son from the dead. Elisha was at Mount Carmel, a journey of about 25 miles. Upon finding him she said, "Did I ask a son of my lord? Did I not say, 'Do not deceive me'?" (2 Kings 4:28).

After sending his servant Gehazi to place his staff alongside the dead son, Elisha returned to the woman's house and prayed for the son. He stretched his body over the corpse twice before resurrection took place.

The reaction of this woman is similar to that of many widows and fatherless children. Because relationship has been ripped from them, they are too frightened to believe God for another relationship. In her anger this woman reminded Elisha that she had told him not to deceive her. When Elisha had given this woman the promise of a son, her response had been, "Do not lie to me." In other words what she was saying was, "This better be for real. Do not get my hopes up only to be dashed. Do not lie to me because I cannot handle the possibility of embracing something I desperately want, only to be devastated by it not happening."

The hope God gives to widows and the fatherless is real. It is, however, understandable that they may be afraid to believe it. When Elijah and Elisha gave these women hope, they both had to stand by what had been promised and believe God to bring life out of death. We must do no less. To give hope to a fragile vessel requires us to stand in faith with her until that hope is realized.

Widows today can be consoled by the fact that others have walked where they have walked. Their predecessors felt the same conflicting emotions, the same angers, fear and grief, and the same tentativeness hindering belief. Because of their faith toward God in small things, God was able to work miracles. He gave them that which was beyond their comprehension. He will do the same for widows today.

Jephthah's Daughter: A Life Set Apart

Judges 11:29–40 tells us about an instance in the life of Jephthah involving his daughter. He vowed (rashly) that if he returned victorious from fighting the Ammonites he would sacrifice to the Lord whatever came through the doors of his house to meet him. Jephthah returned victorious and the first person through his door with timbrel and dancing was his daughter—an only child.

Many assume that Jephthah's daughter was killed. It is also likely, however, that the sacrifice referred to spoke of being given over and devoted completely to the Lord's service, meaning she would be unable to marry or have children. Jephthah's daughter responded to her father by saying, "Do to me according to what has gone out of your mouth" (Judges 11:36). In other words, she chose to embrace the life of celibacy and service imposed on her by her father's vow.

Jephthah's daughter displayed remarkable grace and courage in accepting and embracing this circumstance. Her response is very similar to that which Mary made to the angel Gabriel in Luke 1:38. In ancient Israel women who chose a life of celibacy and service were spoken of as being "widowed" for God.

The thing that impresses me about this story is that both Jephthah and his daughter freely and openly expressed their grief. Jephthah in an open display tore his clothes. He must have been stricken that he had deprived his only daughter of the joy and fulfillment of marriage and motherhood. His daughter asked for two months to go to the hills with her friends to bewail her virginity. Being Jephthah's only child it must have been a great grief to her not to be able to continue the lineage of her father. Each year her friends came to weep with her in her "widowhood."

Sometimes the circumstances of life are unfair and we become victims because of the decisions of others. Jephthah's daughter provides us with a model of courage and sacrifice in facing such circumstances. She may have lost much, but her response caused her to become a biblical model for those who have been through similar circumstances down through the ages. Along with her father, who is listed among the men of faith in Hebrews 11, she must surely be one of God's champions.

Anna the Prophetess: Awaiting the Messiah

The Bible mentions this woman only once. She never left the Temple, giving herself continually to prayer and fasting. This woman was watching and praying for the coming of the Messiah. She rejoiced to see Him the day Mary and Joseph came to the Temple to fulfill the requirements laid down in the Law for purification.

> Now there was one, Anna, a prophetess, the daughter of Phanuel, of the tribe of Asher. She was of a great age, and had lived with a husband seven years from her virginity; and this woman was a widow of about eighty-four years, who did not depart from the temple, but served God with fastings and prayers night and day. And coming in that instant she gave thanks to the Lord, and spoke of Him to all those who looked for redemption in Jerusalem.
>
> Luke 2:36–38

This woman could have remarried, but she chose rather to lay her life down in intercession and worship. This is a unique—and high—call. Some are called to remarriage, others God gifts with celibacy in order to serve Him in the way Anna did. There is no greater thing than to come before the throne of God night and day. Those who come continually before the throne of God are more responsible than we realize in causing His heart to intervene in the affairs of mankind. This woman had such unwavering faith that she ministered faithfully for decades. I believe it is her intercession that helped open the doors for Jesus to come to earth.

Every time God is about to do something of great significance, He finds intercessors to pray His plan through. Anna was one of those people. Could there be any higher call than to intercede for Jesus to come to earth? God is going to use many people, including widows, to birth His end-time purposes through intercession.

The greatest ministry of some widows, whether they are called to remarriage or not, may be the ministry of intercession. God may even ask some of them to remain single for the rest of their lives to better serve Him in this way. Paul refers to these widows in 1 Timothy 5, which we discussed earlier, when he outlines the regulations that determine whether the church is to support a widow or not. Remember, there is no Social Security. A widow has to be supported by her family. If she is over sixty, has been faithful to her husband, has no family and "trusts in God and continues in supplications and prayers night and day . . . [is] well reported for good works: if she has brought up children, if she has lodged strangers, if she has washed the saints' feet, if she has relieved the afflicted, if she has diligently followed every good work," she qualifies for the church to support her (1 Timothy 5:5, 10). Paul says we are to give honor to these widows because they really are in need and also because of the ministry they do.

Anna was a woman of uncommon faith and sacrifice who cried out to God night and day without ceasing. She represents a whole host of people who are called to do the same in our day. Some of the greatest of these, like Anna, will be widows.

Anna demonstrated tenacity in intercession that is uncommon. I believe God is going to use many widows with this level of tenacity for His Church. When Jesus wanted to inspire His followers to persist in intercession, He used the example of a widow. If you are a widow, *you* could be one of them.

160

seventeen

The Two Mites

Jesus said the harvest will be gathered at the end of the age. During this period more souls will come to know Him as Lord and King than at any other time in history. To bring in this harvest God is going to mature the Church to a condition of such unity of purpose and vision that the world will marvel. What part do widows, divorcees and the fatherless have to play in this end-time harvest?

> Now Jesus sat opposite the treasury and saw how the people put money into the treasury. And many who were rich put in much. Then one poor widow came and threw in two mites, which make a quadrans. So He called His disciples to Him and said to them, "Assuredly, I say to you that this poor widow has put in more than all those who have given to the treasury; for they all put in out of their abundance, but she out of her poverty put in all that she had, her whole livelihood."
>
> Mark 12:41–44

161

"What do I have to offer?" a widow may ask. "A couple of mites. A life of brokenness and pain." Such precious souls have as much, if not more, to offer than anyone else. God looks for only one type of vessel: the yielded. If we give Him what we have, no matter how little, He will turn it into more than we could ever imagine. What He is able to do through us is described in Ephesians 3:20 as being "exceedingly abundantly above all that we ask or think."

This widow gave everything she had. Despite the fact that it amounted to little in the natural, Jesus said she gave more. How could this be? I believe there are two reasons. First, she gave sacrificially and, second, she gave in faith. By giving out of her need she demonstrated faith in God that acknowledged Him as her source.

Building the Temple Not Made with Hands

This poor widow gave to the Temple treasury. The Temple represented a religious system that had become corrupt and was about to be destroyed. After Jesus' death and resurrection, the Church became the Temple—God's dwelling place. When you give with faith toward God, you are investing in and helping to build the Temple not made with hands.

The first Temple was built with an enormous amount of sacrifice, always with the vision of providing a dwelling place for God. In this hour God is building a spiritual Temple that will likewise require much sacrifice on our parts along with hearts that are focused and determined to provide Him a dwelling place. Paul comments on this in Ephesians 2:22: ". . . in whom you also are being built together for a dwelling place of God in the Spirit."

I believe widows and the fatherless are going to be instrumental in building the Temple not made with hands. They are going to be an integral part of the end-time army God is raising up. Many of them will remain unknown on earth, but they will be known in heaven as some of God's most faithful and courageous overcomers. I believe the day will come when the Body of Christ will realize the debt we owe to such as these. There are four ways in particular I see God using these champions of faith:

1. *Intercession*. As we have seen, Anna serves as a shining example here. Having no husband or children, she was able to devote herself unreservedly to prayer and fasting. It is interesting that when the Holy Spirit looked for an illustration about tenacity and persistence in prayer, He used the example of a widow. Why is this? Because widows have had to learn to do this just to survive.

2. *Giving*. Widows and the fatherless, more than most, have been tested in the area of trusting God for provision. They have had to learn to give in faith, believing that God would provide when they had nothing. Their two mites could have more impact from heaven's perspective than someone else's millions. I believe that during the harvest many widows are going to show uncommon faith toward God in the area of finances and actually end up financing entire missions and teams by their faith. They are going to be a testimony of God's overwhelming resources for those who trust Him. I believe many of these widows are going to teach others how to break through financially and that people are actually going to come to them and inquire concerning this. Jesus and His disciples were supported by women from their own means (see Luke 8:1–3). Elijah was supported by a widow (see 1 Kings 17) and he

163

is also representative of the end-time ministry God is raising up (see Malachi 4:5–6).

3. *Teams.* God's intention is that the work of ministry be a team effort. The fivefold ministry listed in Ephesians 4 is to work together in teams to equip the Body of Christ for ministry. I believe widows and the fatherless will be integral parts of ministry teams. They will bring a wealth of experience to the teams of which they are a part and will have powerful ministries of restoration. They will be able to relate to a world devastated by the ravages of sin, having the keys and strategies, understanding and wisdom to help them. In a world where increasing darkness and turmoil will exist, these champions will shine as beacons of hope to multitudes of helpless souls. They will also play an integral part in teaching the rest of the Body of Christ to minister in like manner.

4. *Children.* For some, the most important ministry they will have is the raising of children who will play an integral part in God's end-time army. Although many widows may not be known for anything else, they will reap eternal reward through their children.

The New Generation

Finally, let me give the following exhortations to widows who are alone, widows who have children at home and to the fatherless.

Role Models

Dear widow, if your children have left home or you do not have any children, do not let the enemy lie to you and make you feel as though you no longer have a significant contribution to make with the rest of your life. Your prayers for the next generation can have a huge impact on its destiny. You can achieve this by praying for children and their parents.

Your role as a grandma for your own grandchildren or for other children can help to provide security and identity for a largely fatherless generation. Titus 2:3–5 exhorts older women to be godly role models to younger women. Being critical of the next generation is not helpful (see 1 Timothy 5:13). A role model is someone who can be looked to or followed because of her positive influence.

Raising Champions

Dear widow, the children you are raising are destined to be the champions of tomorrow. You may say, "I'm not qualified to raise champions." Who is? Do not let failure or inadequacy stop you from asking for God's wisdom to raise and prepare your children for their God-given destiny. "If any of you lacks wisdom, let him ask of God, who gives to all liberally and without reproach, and it will be given to him" (James 1:5).

God wants you to see your children's spiritual inheritance and destiny. You may know your natural children in the flesh, but ask Him to show you who they are in the Spirit and how you can best nurture and train them. For some this avenue of help and wisdom seems blocked off because they are overwhelmed with guilt at the wrongs they have done. We have all made mistakes. Plenty of them. "For we all stumble in many things" (James 3:2).

Don't let condemnation prevent you from seeking the help you need now. You cannot change the past but you can change the future. Your worth does not come from your parenting. Your worth comes from being a child of God, wonderfully and fearfully made. God loves you; to Him you are beautiful. The Bible says He loved you while you were a sinner; how much more now that you are one of His own children!

It *is* really tough parenting alone. That is reality. But remember, God plus one is a majority. God will use your struggles to inspire faith in your children. You can be a testimony to them by succeeding against overwhelming odds. Instead of being victims, they can become champions who have a testimony imprinted on their hearts from a mother who chose to have courage even when she felt like the least courageous of all. Widow, you have a lot to offer. Do not let the enemy rob you. His plan is to render you ineffective through condemnation.

A Significant Role

If you are part of this fatherless generation, God wants you to see yourself through His eyes. The struggles you have had to go through are possibly greater than those of any previous generation. It is obvious that Satan has tried to destroy you through abortion, rejection and family breakdown before you even got a chance. The biggest lie he has sowed into the minds of your generation is that you have no purpose or destiny. He has tried to preoccupy your minds and wear you down with the struggle of twenty-first-century living—a struggle that involves above all else a quest for significance.

Champions come out of the midst of difficult circumstances and situations. Satan's biggest fear is that this fatherless generation will see the awesome call of God on their lives and rise up with vengeance to destroy his works and deceptions. Like the widow with only two small coins, what you have may seem small, but it is significant—very significant. Because of what you have missed out on, you will be entrusted to carry revelations of the Father.

The reason God is able to do this is because He knows you will treasure and esteem these revelations above all else. You play a vital part in His end-time strategy and are called to reveal to the world that God is "a father of the fatherless, a defender of widows" (Psalm 68:5). Surely you will be able to say with David, "When my father and my mother forsake me, then the LORD will take care of me" (Psalm 27:10).

eighteen

From Reproach to Honor

"Sing, O barren, you who have not borne! Break forth into singing, and cry aloud, you who have not labored with child! For more are the children of the desolate than the children of the married woman," says the LORD. "Enlarge the place of your tent, and let them stretch out the curtains of your dwellings; do not spare; lengthen your cords, and strengthen your stakes. For you shall expand to the right and to the left, and your descendants will inherit the nations, and make the desolate cities inhabited. Do not fear, for you will not be ashamed; neither be disgraced, for you will not be put to shame; for you will forget the shame of your youth, and will not remember the reproach of your widowhood anymore. For your Maker is your husband, the LORD of hosts is His name; and your Redeemer is the Holy One of Israel; He is called the God of the whole earth. For the LORD has called you like a woman forsaken and grieved in spirit, like a youthful wife when you were refused," says your God.

Isaiah 54:1–6

The Hebrew word for *reproach* used in Isaiah 54:4 comes from a primary root meaning "to pull off, to expose as if by stripping." Can God heal such reproach? The Bible says not only that He can, but also that He will.

The following imaginary story shows how God takes broken vessels, those shattered by reproach, and restores them to dignity and honor.

The Two Vessels

Before me were two earthenware vessels. The one on the left lay smashed and broken. Fragments were everywhere. The one on the right stood tall and stately. It was beautiful to behold, a vessel obviously shaped by a master craftsman. The perfection and beauty of this vessel was breathtaking. Its colors ran together, displaying every tint and shade imaginable. It must have taken hours of skilled and intricate work to make. As I turned my gaze back to the shattered fragments of the other vessel, something stirred in my heart.

"Lord, why do these broken pieces of clay give me this weird, uneasy feeling?"

I studied the fragments carefully, trying to figure it out. Finally I could bear it no longer. I did not like what I was feeling. My gaze was riveted to the vessel of perfection and beauty. It gave me a sense of rest and peace. The broken pieces, however, would not leave me alone. It was as though they were trying to communicate something. I made a pretense of looking away, but in my curiosity I continued to view them out of the corner of my eye. How could inanimate pieces of clay have so much life? I was mystified and somewhat perplexed.

"God, tell these pieces of clay to leave me alone."

The Broken Fragments

In a final attempt to appease my curiosity, I turned my gaze back to the broken shards. Each piece of clay seemed somehow familiar. Each represented something, and whatever that something was, I was feeling strongly empathetic toward it. Each fragment I studied seemed to come to life, pulling me into some mystery it revealed. It was unbelievable, like entering into another world.

The scenes were not pleasant—in fact, they were somewhat disturbing, but after viewing—or should I say entering into—a few of them, a shocking realization came. They were events from my own life.

This clay vessel represented me! Frantically I went from piece to piece, terrified of what the next fragment might reveal, until it became too overwhelming to continue. The pain in my heart was piercing. This couldn't be my life; it couldn't be true.

"Please, God, don't let it be true."

Shame engulfed me.

"God, don't look at me. I'm so unworthy."

I could hear the reproach of others. Voices, so many voices. Voices from the past echoing and resounding in my mind.

"God, why did I ever look at those clay pieces?"

I felt surrounded, and everyone was looking at me. The sense of exposure was tormenting. The reproach coming toward me was suffocating. In desperation I tried frantically to pick up all the broken fragments and hide them so no one could see. I felt as though people were throwing stones at me; I doubled over in pain.

"God, they're sucking the very life out of me. Get me out of this house of murder."

The pain stopped and the scene ended. Dull gray pieces of inanimate clay stared back at me.

The Man

Dazed by what had just happened, I looked up to see a Man approaching. He was of ordinary appearance but had a warm, open demeanor about Him. He got down on His hands and knees and began picking up all the many fragments of clay that represented my life. When He had gathered all the pieces, He placed them on a table and began piecing them back together. He worked slowly and patiently with focus and determination written on His face.

As each piece of fragmented clay was joined to another, painful scenes erupted from within. There were so many fragmented sections of my heart, it was too overwhelming to consider. This Master Craftsman, however, knew how much I could take at one time and focused on that one area for as long as it took to accomplish the healing.

At times, when it was too much for me, He would relax and just look at me, loving me. No matter whether He was working or relaxed, He always communicated love and security. His eyes were so warm and beautiful! Hidden within them were vision and destiny such as I had never known. He had so much vision for me it strengthened me.

Some fragments of clay were sharp. Though He placed them together carefully, delicately, still the pain was excruciating and sometimes I lashed out at Him. He had many cuts on His fingers from handling those pieces of clay. Often I would want to give up and forget the entire painful process.

One day in particular I decided I could go on no longer. The pain in my heart had become unbearable, or so I thought. It was causing me to question the Man's love for me. Finally, in a rage, I tore myself away from His hands.

"How can this be love? Don't touch me. Leave me alone."

I felt relief at having released myself from the Man's grip. I could see a fresh cut on His fingers. It looked deep and painful. It surprised me that He didn't pick me up and smash me into a million pieces with those strong hands. Still, I did not feel any remorse. I was convinced I could sort out my own life and go about it in a much more humane way.

Looking back at the Man's face I saw such pain and grief I almost broke down weeping, but caught myself in time and hardened my heart.

"What do You know about pain? You don't understand."

I turned away, defiant.

The Useless Vessel

After days of trying to go it alone I found myself exhausted, confused and in more pain than before. In desperation I cried out to God.

"Help me, God, I'm dying and alone."

The Lord opened my eyes and I saw a clay pot in the distance. This was not what I wanted to see. It had associations I would rather have forgotten.

The clay vessel looked whole. Well, that at least was a relief. I felt prompted to approach the clay vessel and so started walking. It was not until I drew closer that I realized the vessel had been glued together. It was not a whole vessel after all. Many pieces were still missing. I realized the Lord was speaking to me.

This clay vessel looked whole from a distance but in reality it was useless and could hold nothing. The message was becoming clear. It represented what I was trying to do. Because of my sense of shame and exposure, I had tried to make it look as though I had everything all together. It was my attempt to mend my broken heart. How utterly useless! The realization hit me.

"God, forgive me for turning away from You and breaking Your heart. I surrender my life to You. I'm sorry, Lord, for accusing You of being a cruel taskmaster; I know You are not. Forgive me for my rebellion."

Consumed with Him

Once again I submitted to the Craftsman and let Him continue to piece the broken fragments of my heart together. Because of what I had been through, I determined to make it as easy as I could for the Craftsman. Still, it was not easy, but each area that was healed became another victory I could celebrate.

Most precious of all was the experience I had of coming to know the Craftsman. In the midst of the pain, when my heart was raw and tender, I had come to seek solace in Him. He was becoming my most intimate and precious Friend. There were still many things I did not understand, but as time went on I began to trust Him more and more. Sometimes we would laugh together and lovingly tease one another. It was a relief to be able to see the funny side of the process. I became more and more absorbed with Him.

"Jesus, whether I'm whole or broken, it doesn't matter, I just want to be with You. I want to love You with every atom and fiber of my being."

What others thought of me and how others saw me were now of no importance. As He became the supreme obsession of my heart, nothing else mattered.

The Colorful Vessel

Time passed, and one day a memory stirred. I had become so focused on watching the Master repair the broken vessel that I had forgotten the other beautifully colored vessel that once stood beside it.

I found myself in front of a table holding the two vessels. There was the patched vessel on the left and the masterpiece on the right. The stunning colors and beautiful glaze captured and gripped my heart. Suddenly I realized the truth: It was I, as I had now become. I looked closely, and in every place where there had been a fracture or break, there was now a beautiful blend and mix of colors. The places of brokenness had been transformed to give the vessel its beauty and most vibrant color. I remembered the broken pieces of dull unglazed clay and saw with great delight how He had taken away the reproach of my abandonment and neglect!

The Last Battle

There is reserved in heaven a seat of honor for those who overcome (see Revelation 3:21). In eternity some of the greatest overcomers will have come from the ranks of those who were widowed and fatherless. In the last great battle at the end of the age, their courage will strengthen others, causing the lines not only to hold but to advance. As the Body of Christ we will need the revelations they carry. Widows and the fatherless will be instrumental in freeing multitudes from the reproach of the enemy. Not only are they called to be overcomers themselves, but they are to cause many others to be overcomers. The Lord is about to remove the reproach of those who have been dishonored and despised.

He shall regard the prayer of the destitute,
And shall not despise their prayer.
This will be written for the generation to come,
That a people yet to be created may praise the LORD.
For He looked down from the height of His sanctuary;
From heaven the LORD viewed the earth,
To hear the groaning of the prisoner,
To release those appointed to death.

Psalm 102:17–20

A cry has gone up before His throne. He is about to release the prisoners from their heavy chains. Now is the time. He will not delay.

In 1998 Nathan Shaw founded Heart of David Ministries with the following four mandates.

1. Continuous worship and intercession
2. Sending out prophetic and apostolic teams to the nations
3. Restoration for men, women, children, divorcees, widows and the fatherless
4. Release of divine creativity

Nathan is a writer, itinerant preacher, missionary and piano teacher. His heart is for the Body of Christ to be healed, strengthened, equipped and ignited through fresh encounters with the living God. He conducts seminars and Holy Spirit Encounter meetings both locally and internationally. Nathan lives in Mosgiel, New Zealand.

The Heart of David Ministries website has information on "The Call" prayer meetings, Holy Spirit Encounter meetings, Eagle Training schools, seminars and missions trips, as well as timely prophetic articles.

For more information please feel free to contact:

Heart of David Ministries
31 Lanark St.
Mosgiel
New Zealand
www.heartofdavidministries.org